MOTHERHOOD'S NOT FOR PUNKS

A Badass Mom's Guide To Self Mastery, Mindful Mothering And Having It All When You Do It All

PATRINA WISDOM

Motherhood's Not for Punks

by Patrina Wisdom
Cover Design by Colleen Davis
Front Cover Photo by Andrew Reed Photography
Back Cover Photo by Jerry Metellus Photography
Copyright © 2015 by Patrina Wisdom

ISBN: 978-1-944177-15-7 (e)
ISBN: 978-1-944177-16-4 (p)

Crescendo Publishing, LLC
300 Carlsbad Village Drive
Ste. 108A, #443
Carlsbad, California 92008-2999

www.CrescendoPublishing.com
GetPublished@CrescendoPublishing.com

A Gift from the Author
STOP!

https://youtu.be/vo443Zuf5kM

As my way of saying thank you for your purchase of this book, I am gifting you with a complimentary download of my
Awakening Life Audio and many more yummy bonuses.

In this audio I will take you on a journey to:

- Awaken Your Self-Esteem
- Awaken Your Creativity
- Awaken Your True Self

Download NOW at:
www.MotherhoodsNotforPunks.com/bonuses

What Are People Saying?

Patrina, thank you for my fresh start! I needed this Awakening Life course at this very moment! This is the beginning of a new chapter for me and I'm happy that you're here helping me to write the story. Thank you for stepping into your purpose so that I can finally step into mine without fear, hesitation or any other limiting thoughts. I appreciate you.

—Marisha Dixon, M Street TV

Patrina is a life changer! I came to her at a pivotal point in my life, where I was at [a] cross roads in my personal life, and looking to start a business. Patrina rescued me from that scared, confused, frustrated person I had become and awakened the true me. Through her powerful coaching, I emerged on the other side with more clarity, deeper vision, and a mission to fulfill my financial, personal, and spiritual destiny. Thanks to you, my firm was born. I have two lovely kids. And I am living the mom-preneur lifestyle.

—Augusta Massey, Esq., Massey & Associates Law Firm

I had the pleasure of working with Patrina as a coach during the beginning of my career transition and she helped me realize not only my worth and value in what I wanted to do (fitness and educating others on compassionate living), but that by being gentle with myself (quiet time, crazy dance, journaling, massage, pet therapy, bf time, yoga, meditation, etc.) each day brings more peace and balance to my life. And it has! I'm not so strung out and overwhelmed.

—Melissa V. Andrews, Purposed Hands
Virtual Assisting & Online Business Manager

I truly believe that when you trust in God, He will bring you what you need when you need it. I discovered Patrina Wisdom and her coaching services right at the time when I was trying to recreate my life. I was ready to make some major changes, but was unsure and quite frankly scared to do so. In my coaching sessions with Patrina, I am learning to be more deliberate and intentional in my actions to have the lifestyle that I desire. Patrina has helped me to be more focused and confident so that I can boldly pursue my innermost dreams and make them a reality for my life.

–DeAndre Green

Since my divorce, I have [had] major life changes that I did not know how to handle for the most part. Patrina has been able to guide me in such a positive direction. I have learned more about myself than I have known my entire life. I have regained my power as a woman, mother and business owner.

–Alexandra Lee

In Dedication

First and foremost, this book is dedicated to the Divine Spirit that guides, carries, and works through me. I would not be the person I am, doing all the things that I am doing, without the grace, love, guidance, and mercy of Source.

This book is dedicated to ME—a woman who had the courage to answer and honor her call to divine, authentic, feminine leadership. A woman who, despite all her insecurities, challenges, and fears, continuously moves mountains to be the light for others. A woman who has learned to love herself, and others, unconditionally.

This book is a dedication to the love of my life, Mr. Alexander Damon Green, with whom I shared the most important love and learned the most important lessons in this lifetime. We promised "till death do us part," and we fulfilled that promise. Over the years I've learned how to live without your physical presence, but I will never let go of or forget the love that we shared. You are and will always be my rock.

This book is dedicated to anyone (male or female) who has loved and lost. For some, the love that has been lost is the love of another; for others the love that has been lost is the love of self. You have everything you need. This book will help you rediscover yourself, and once you do, never lose sight of who you really are ever again. Never again allow your life circumstances to define you or make you feel unworthy.

"Many have tried and failed, but what makes you a hero is that you keep on trying."

– Patrina Wisdom

Contents

Introduction

My name is Patrina Wisdom, and much like you, I have had a life filled with all kinds of experiences, some of them incredible and some of them not so great. I am a survivor of heartbreak, disappointment, molestation, rape, personal loss, financial hardship, divorce, single parenting, promiscuity, Shaming, and many other traumas. I am you! I embody and share the collective experience of the community, and I am honored to have the opportunity to share my story—and my Wisdom—with you.

Your decision to read this book tells me that you have been navigating the jarring twists and turns that life often brings and that you have recently hit a wall, a crossroad that is forcing you to take a look at your life from a different perspective and make some decisions.

Maybe it's in your work: you're a mom looking to start a career, change careers, or move up in your career. Maybe you are questioning your purpose or want to gain more control over your time and your life. Maybe you're a single mom looking for a relationship, looking to leave a relationship, or trying to improve a relationship. Perhaps you're having health issues that are making you question your mental, spiritual, emotional, and physical habits. You may be struggling with an addiction or have completely lost sight of who you are and what you want. Maybe you've recently been laid off or lost your main source of financial support in a divorce or the death of a partner, and you are wondering, what's next? Are you feeling stifled and frustrated or like you're dimming your light to keep those around you comfortable? Are you putting motherhood or another role that you play in your life ahead of your own well-being? If so, it's time to STOP!

1

Maybe you want to open up your creativity or explore possibilities for entrepreneurship. You've been dreaming of starting a business but can't decide what to do or where to start. Maybe you are feeling less than fulfilled in a relationship and need guidance on how to change it or the courage to get out of it. Maybe you're struggling with self-esteem, questioning your purpose, feeling overwhelmed, or maybe you just want to learn how to maintain balance in your life. Maybe you know who you are, but you're apprehensive about showing your true self to others for fear of what they may think.

You are a visionary. You're tenacious and driven. You know deep down in your soul that there is more for you to BE in the world, but you have a deep-rooted fear of inadequacy— feelings of not being "enough" or maybe being "too much." For one reason or another you are seeking change. You know that you need to try something new, but you don't know where to start. Your current situation or circumstances have you doubting yourself, your decision making, your abilities, and your future.

Well, here is the good news: when the student is ready, the teacher appears. It's time to get back in the driver's seat and "awaken your life!" You are not alone. The hardest part of making change happen in your life is twofold: making the decision to do so and then committing to the process. The process of "Awakening Life" is not for everyone! It's only for those who are ready to change their perspective, change their habits, and try new things.

Are you ready to improve your relationships, make more money, and have more fulfillment in your career and in your life? Are you ready to own ALL parts of yourself, find your unique voice, and live as a fully expressed woman and mother? This book is for those of you who are ready to open up and explore these possibilities, those of you who want to have more effective habits that will allow you to think clearer, make better decisions, and accomplish things that you never knew you could.

As a single mother of four children and a successful mompreneur, I understand how easy it is to lose yourself in your roles. I understand the unique challenges of being an empowered woman and mother while also maintaining a career. I also understand the challenges that come along with being a stay-at-home mom (that was my reality for years). It can be a real balancing act, and many moms have a hard time finding the tools, support, and community that they need. My intention for this book is to walk you through my 6 Step Wisdom Process for Awakening Life, and support you as you "take off the masks" so that you can embody and live as the most Badass Bodacious version of yourself.

This is your life, and you get only one shot. Do you want to unblock your potential and unleash possibilities that will allow you to have your perfect mate, your dream life, exotic vacations, or a career that you would wake up every morning and do even if you weren't getting paid? Do you want to live a Badass Bodacious Life? If so, then I am talking to you! You are ready to change from limiting beliefs, habits, and thoughts to empowered action that will improve your quality of life.

This book was written for you.

Chapter 1

My Story

-1-

My Story

When people see me, they see a woman who appears to have it all! A leader. A woman with grace, charisma, a positive spirit, and magnetism that lights up the room. A woman who's always on the move, traveling, happy, and living her dreams.

What they don't see is ME. A woman with a story. A woman with scars, issues, fears, and insecurities. What they don't see is "The woman behind the mask."

My story begins on November 8, 1973, when I was born to an unwed teenage mother in Las Vegas, Nevada.

Unlike the typical teenage-mom stereotypes, I was born into a relationship of love and union. My mom and dad were never married, and they had a huge gap in age and maturity, but they were in love and living their life together.

So it was painful to witness the slow, steady demise of my parents' relationship. During the years that my mom and dad (our family) were together, I witnessed my mom struggle with loneliness within the relationship, mutual abuse (mental and physical), deception, lies, and disconnection.

My dad left for work at five every morning and didn't return home from work until eight in the evening. When he came home, he would shower, eat, watch some TV, and go to bed. On the weekends he would read the paper and watch TV, or he would go out and place bets on games; I never saw a real connection between him and my mother, and there was no real connection established between us either. He was physically present but emotionally absent. I never had the opportunity to get to know him and therefore felt like a fatherless child.

His role or "mask" that he wore was the "Provider Mask." It was his belief that his job was to provide for his family, and that was the only way that he knew how to show his love. His love was directly related to duty; therefore, his ability to connect intimately with me, my mother, or anyone else for that matter, was sadly underdeveloped.

My mom spent her days watching soap operas and talking on the phone because, for the most part, what she yearned for was connection. She also worked outside the home as a waitress, cocktail server, and/or ring girl for the big Las Vegas fights where she got lots of attention, validation, and social interaction. My mom was beautiful and charming, which also made her very vulnerable. She was young and naive, and she was not being taken care of emotionally at home, so it was easy for trouble to find her.

Contrary to my dad's personality, where he had trouble expressing love, my mom recklessly gave love without boundaries or thought of consequence. She wore the "See Me, Love Me Mask," so it was no surprise that deception, infidelity, and abuse came into play in the relationship (on both sides), which created turbulence and chaos at home.

Although I had my own room in our home at the time, I still never felt safe in my own home because in the midst of my parents' chaotic relationship, one of my male cousins came to live with us while his mom (another young single mother) went off to pursue a modeling and acting career in New York City. He had a world of pain and anger that he was dealing with in his own way, which I often became the victim of.

He was hurt because his dad wasn't in his life, and in his mind his mom had also abandoned him. He held the perception that I had the perfect life because my mom and dad were living together in a nice home. He wanted what he thought I had, and I was continuously punished for it. He tormented me with words like stupid, spoiled, ugly, and selfish—words that would take years to rid from my psyche. Over time, his behaviors with us became increasingly physically aggressive, overpowering, and outright abusive.

At night he would sneak into my bed, claiming to be afraid to sleep alone. In an effort to avoid conflict, I'd let him stay, which in his mind also gave him permission to touch me in ways he'd seen adults touching, both in movies and in real life. No amount of resistance was enough to make him stop. I felt helpless, and all I could do was be quiet and let it happen. I lost my personal power and my voice before it ever developed. My shame around our behaviors and fear of getting in trouble or causing more chaos amongst the family kept me quiet. I wore the mask of "The Good Girl," and I did whatever it took to keep the peace.

I also understood on some level that my cousin felt helpless, that he was hurting, and that he could not control the circumstances of his life or process and manage the emotions he was feeling. So I became the sponge for his pain. I allowed him to treat me as his property and control me, all the while telling me how much he loved me. It was a very confusing and unhealthy relationship, but we became very close during this time because we were family, we loved each other deeply, and the fact is that we were in it together.

I tried to tell my mom about the abuse I was experiencing, but my experience was not validated and I didn't feel protected. On the contrary, his behavior was defended and justified because of the pain he was experiencing. But what about my pain?

By age six I had already developed the belief that other people's experiences and emotions were more important than mine and that love came with consequence and responsibility. I felt unworthy of love unless I did something to deserve it: "get good grades," "clean your room," "get along," "let me touch your pussy" ... you know, stuff like that. I learned how to be a pleaser. I had developed a deep-rooted belief that I was not "enough." No one ever told me I wasn't enough. I formed this belief as a result of the feedback I witnessed.

I felt unsafe and insecure, so I put all my toys into my closet and created an imaginary cave for myself, a safe space in an imaginary land with imaginary friends. It was my escape from the pain and uncertainty of life. It was the one place I could go to find peace. There I played happily for hours at a time, hoping and praying that no one would come looking for me.

A year or so later, right around 1980, my dad sent my mom and me to New York City to visit my aunt and cousin who, by that time, had gone back to live with his mother. While we were there, a well-known modeling agency discovered my mom, and the opportunities started pouring in, so we ended up staying in New York City.

Overnight we went from living in a nice, big house in Las Vegas with my dad, to living in a tiny, one-bedroom, rat-infested New York City apartment with my aunt and cousin, often with no heat in the winter and very little food. The move was sudden, unexplained, and uncomfortable. Oh, how the tables had turned. I was now the visitor in my cousin's home sharing a room with him. I later found out that the tickets my dad bought to send us to New York were one-way tickets.

My life was forever changed, and I was forced to grow up and change with it. Over the next few years we frequently moved from borough to borough and apartment to apartment. I learned very quickly how to adapt to any environment, how to play well with others, and how to take care of myself.

Initially, the sudden absence of my father seemed to affect little, other than our finances. It didn't seem to matter if he was 3,000 miles away or in the same room because either way he felt emotionally inaccessible to me. No matter how much I tried, I was unsuccessful at connecting with my father, and things got even worse while we lived in New York. I often wondered why I talked to my dad only when I called him. I acted like I didn't care, but deep down it hurt me so deeply to think that my own father didn't think enough of me to call and check on me.

Things went from bad to worse in 1984 when I tried calling my dad to check in with him like I always did, and his phone number was disconnected. I knew that he and my mom were having problems, but I guess I didn't realize how bad it was. As a child I had no concept of time, and apparently neither did my mom—who was living in the delusion that she and my dad were still together, even though we had been living 3,000 miles away for the last four years. Her delusion was quickly shattered, though, after my dad's sister called to let us know that my dad had recently gotten married and changed his phone number.

This was a major blow to my self-worth and self-esteem that sent me over the edge, and I started acting on an overwhelming desire for external validation—validation that I believed (at that time) could be found only in a man. My craving for male attention had me out running the streets of NYC at all hours of the night, putting myself in potentially dangerous situations. It was my way of escaping the pain of feeling unwanted by my dad. I was now wearing the "See Me, Love Me Mask" that my mom had previously worn.

I was so obsessed with feeling desired that I found myself submitting to the desires of men without question. I didn't speak up for myself, I had no clear boundaries, and I lost my ability to say NO (which is a complete sentence, by the way). My commitment to avoiding conflict and feeling desired put me into a position to be molested, raped, and taken advantage of time and time again.

My mom was so devastated by the news of my dad's marriage that she fell into a depression for three years. She was so out of it that she couldn't work, couldn't show up for herself or for me. Then in 1988—in the middle of my junior year, two intense auditions, and being accepted to LaGuardia High School for the Performing Arts—my mom announced that we were moving back to Las Vegas. I begged and pleaded to stay in New York with family and continue pursuing my dreams of being on Broadway, but my mother needed me. I was all she had, and she wasn't leaving without me. She had exhausted her masks and could no longer run away from or mask her pain.

Upon our return to Las Vegas, I took on two and three jobs to help support the household because my mom still hadn't recovered from the grief of losing her relationship with my father. One of my jobs was as a hostess at the University of Las Vegas dining commons where I fed the students and athletes. It was there that I met the most beautiful, confident, charismatic man I'd ever seen. I had to have him.

I knew in my heart of hearts from the first moment I saw him that he would be my husband. As cliché as it sounds, it really was love at first sight. So like everything else in my life, once I decided that I wanted him, I put on my "Seductress Mask" and I made it happen.

Chapter 2

The Turning Point

-2-

The Turning Point

Fast-forward twenty years and three children later, to the morning of January 6, 2009. It was a typical Tuesday morning. We woke up; rolled over; expressed our gratitude for each other, our life, and our beautiful family; and then we playfully got ready for the day ahead. We then headed downstairs to have breakfast together as a family (like we did on most days).

Every day together was like a fairy tale. The sun was shining, birds were chirping, and a beautiful score was playing in the back of my head every day, knowing that I had a man who loved me, a lifestyle that people dreamed about, and three of the most beautiful, intelligent children that anyone had ever met. My entire identity was tied to our perfect little family.

We were often compared to people who grace the covers of publications like *Black Enterprise* magazine and *Essence*. Friends teased that we were the Will Smith and Jada Pinkett Smith of the real world (and I loved it). It had taken years of hard work and emotional ups and downs to get there, but we had finally arrived. We had it all (or so I thought).

After breakfast, I walked my husband to the door, adjusted his tie, praised him for how handsome he looked, told him how awesome he was as a father and a husband, and kissed him good-bye (as I did every morning). Then I went about my day as usual, but this Tuesday would prove to be anything but.

This was the day that I would find out for sure if I was pregnant with our fourth child as we suspected I might be. I anxiously hurried to get the kids dressed and off to school so that I wouldn't be late for my appointment with Dr. Bourgault.

"Mrs. Green, Dr. Bourgault is ready for you."

"Oh thanks … I'll be right there."

As I entered the office—my stomach tied up in knots—the bright, friendly smiles on the staffs' faces meant to provide comfort provoked the opposite response … one of horror and disgust. This year had been hard enough as we'd tried to maintain our lifestyle and recover our losses from the last year. We, like many other Americans, took a financial hit during the mortgage crisis in 2008 and were feeling stressed and overwhelmed as a result.

We already had three children, only one of which was planned. What the fuck were we going to do if I was pregnant again? As I gripped the plastic cup and entered the ladies' room, I rolled my eyes and cursed my husband for jokingly saying he was going to get me pregnant before making love the month before. Then I said a quick prayer for the results to be negative.

As I sat in that small, cold, sterile examination room, time seemed to have stopped, and I began to notice every little detail about the room: uneven tiles, chipped paint, and my ass sticking to the paper that lined the examination table. My heart was pounding out of my chest. "What's taking her so long to come in with my results? That can't be a good sign."

Impatiently I waited as I struggled to distract myself from the thoughts of how different life would look with a fourth child, and I wondered how my husband would take the news. We'd suspected for weeks that pregnancy was a possibility. (After all, we did spend the last month or so warming each other up by seeing who would tap out first in the bedroom. We'd had quite the lovemaking marathon.) Just as I began drifting into the sweet memories of our sweaty sessions, the doctor walked in with my results.

"Hello, Mrs. Green. How are you today?"

"Fine," I replied.

"Well, congratulations! You are indeed pregnant."

As I sat in my car with my head pressed firmly into the steering wheel, tears began tickling my cheeks. Excited and afraid, I reached for my purse and pulled out my cell phone to share the news about the pregnancy with my husband. I wanted him to reassure me that everything would be okay.

The financial hit that we took affected my husband much more than it did me because a man's pride is so closely tied to his income and how he provides for his family. Like my father, he took pride in wearing "The Provider Mask."

I spent countless days and nights reassuring him that I loved him no matter what we did or didn't have, and that even if we lost everything, it wouldn't matter because we had each other. We were a great team, and I knew that if we built it once and lost it, that we could always build it again. I was never tied to the material things and he knew it, but unfortunately, his sense of self, identity, and manhood was tied to it.

With the touch of each button, my heartbeat quickened. Ring ... Ring ... Ring ... and then straight to voice mail.

I had to admit, I was kind of relieved as I left a message.

"Hey babe, I just left the doctor's office. Call me ASAP. I will also text you."

Many completed errands and hours later I realized that I'd sent several texts and left several messages for my husband and still had no answer. That was odd because he always took my calls and always got back to me pretty quickly.

A few hours later I tried calling him again, but this time his voice mail was full, so I called his office. The receptionist cheerfully greeted me.

"Hello, Mrs. Green. Good to hear from you. Is Alex okay? He hasn't been to the office in over a month. We were starting to worry about him."

My heart stopped for at least ten seconds before I replied, "Yes, he's fine." I told her that we had been traveling over the holidays and spending quality time together as a family, which was true by the way. It had been one of the best holiday seasons we'd ever had, and my husband seemed to be the happiest he had ever been.

Despite my panic and utter confusion, I could do nothing but smile and act like everything was okay. I went about my day picking up the kids from school, making dinner, doing homework, and even putting the finishing touches on my daughter's thirteenth birthday celebration that I was planning for the following evening—all the while optimistically waiting for my best friend and lover of over twenty years to walk through the door. Once the kids went down for bed and all the distractions ceased, I sat crying and waiting, waiting and crying.

My secret hope was that my gut feeling was wrong and that I would wake up the next morning and find my husband lying next to me in a drunken slumber. But no. Instead, I woke to find a business card on my front door from the Las Vegas coroner's office with a note to call them immediately.

As I picked up the phone to dial the coroner's office, I gagged on the huge lump in my throat. My husband had been missing for twenty-four hours, I had just found out that I was pregnant with my fourth child, and no matter what they were about to tell me, I had a thirteenth birthday party to host for my daughter that evening.

When the operator answered, I took a deep breath … and then I told them who I was. They informed me that my husband had been found dead in his Jeep on the side of the road up at Mount Charleston, with a self-inflicted gunshot to the chest. They needed me to come down and identify the body.

It hit me like a brick: in that moment, on January 6, 2009, I watched my husband, the man I championed and built my entire life around for over twenty years, grab his briefcase, kiss his family good-bye, and walk out the door, knowing that he would never return.

I had been a stay-at-home mom for years, embracing the role of supporter because I was timid about my own power and self-conscious about my beauty. I struggled with feelings of not only being "not enough" but of also being "too much." I believed that I needed to be protected, and I didn't mind being the woman behind the man. So I put my own dreams and talents on the back burner, and I built my entire identity around my family, allowing my overachieving, type-A personality husband to take the wheel and set the tone for our family.

As my life flashed before me, all I could think about was why did he do it? What pushed him to choose to leave the kids and me? How would I explain this to the children? What long-lasting effects would this have on them? I was heartbroken and felt completely betrayed and abandoned. Every deep-rooted fear, issue, and insecurity that I ever had rose to greet me.

I began to question whether our entire twenty years together had been a lie. My husband and I had set very strict standards for our children and worked hard to instill a culture of high achievement in our home. For the first time I started to question whether imposing these unrealistic standards on our kids and modeling a lifestyle of overachievement was healthy for our kids. My husband held himself and us to a standard of excellence that he himself was not able to live up to. I began to wonder if it was these types of unrealistic expectations and standards that drove him to do what he did, and if so, how was this lifestyle affecting our children?

Our family code of honor that hung proudly on our wall was built on honesty, courage, always being your best, and never giving up. In my eyes that was exactly what he had done – he had given up not only on himself but on his partner and family.

Either way you look at it, my children would no longer have a father to support, guide, and protect them. I would no longer have my lover and best friend to share my life with. The security, unconditional love, and support I'd become accustomed to was now gone, and I was left to pick up the pieces while raising four children on my own. I was alone, and for the first time in years I felt hopeless, helpless, lost, and confused. But I also had enough love and compassion for my husband to know that he had to have been in an incredible amount of pain to rip himself out of our lives the way that he did, and that there was a greater purpose for our loss. And perhaps he had made the ultimate sacrifice for his family.

Chapter 3

The Masks We Wear

-3-

The Masks We Wear

As women and mothers, there is so much pressure to be everything to everybody that we often become a slave to the expectations that we've placed on ourselves. For the sake of the story, I will call these self-imposed expectations and roles "masks." We have all worn these masks at one time or another, and it's important to recognize what masks you wear so that you can work on shedding them later in the book.

For almost a year I made it my personal mission to not let my husband's death be in vain. I wanted to prove to myself—and others—that I could do it alone. I had been raised in a family of strong, independent, single mothers, so I had no doubt in my mind that I could make it without a man, but that was the very pattern I had worked so hard to break. I chose to be submissive, I chose to get married, and I chose to stick it out "until death do us part." I wanted to be the one who broke the curse of young single mothers in my family. I chose to be the one who owned a home so that my family would always have somewhere soft to land. I very consciously created my reality. But in the blink of an eye, that reality was ripped out from under me.

Aside from a few private rumblings in the dead of the night, I put my grief and pain on hold for the sake of my three—soon to be four—children and everyone else around me because I felt a responsibility to be strong for them.

I had many people around me offering condolences and support, but true to form, I felt a responsibility to put on my "Caretaker Mask" and comfort them instead of honoring my own experience. I recognized that my tragedy was also their tragedy, and that they were suffering with the same pain, anger, and confusion that I was.

My feelings of unworthiness ran so deep that I completely robbed myself of the opportunity to be held, loved, and supported. I felt like it really wasn't about me. At that time in my life, I didn't have the capacity to receive care, compassion, and sympathy from others because I didn't have care, compassion, or sympathy for myself. I was so worried about being seen as a "victim" or coming off as weak that I completely ignored the rumblings of despair that were erupting inside me. I also felt a responsibility to pick up the pieces and fill the void that my husband left in their lives. (Crazy, huh?)

We had worked so hard to secure our roles as leaders in the community and supporters to our friends, colleagues, and family members. So despite my own fears, grief, and feelings of displacement, it was my programming to put on my "Superwoman Mask" and make everything better (ta-da!). I felt responsible for their loss, and I also felt a compelling need to protect the "image" of my now-dead husband (yep, I really said that).

What choice did I have? This was the culture that WE had created, the code that we lived by. How could I possibly go against the philosophies and the way of being that WE had modeled for so long? It was the perfect picture of SUCCESS by society's standards (and look where that got us). I didn't have the luxury of falling apart the way everyone else did because I was now a slave to the "Mask of Perfection" that we had worn for so long.

Within two weeks of my husband's death, so as not to inconvenience his teammates or his clients (heaven forbid), I put on my "Savior Mask" and made the decision to take over my husband's financial business. I did not want anyone to be disappointed or angry with him (the dead man), so I continued to protect and defend him for almost two years after his death, and I fully embraced his role as the "The Machine" (yet another mask). I was always first in the office and last out, fully embracing my late husband's unrelenting appetite for success. There were no weekends or holidays for me. The philosophy we had lived by was "you can sleep when you die." If that was our hardcore philosophy before my husband's passing, you can imagine how much more pressure I was feeling to perform now.

Remember that I was also pregnant. So by becoming this "Machine," I was neglecting my health, my family, my friends, my unborn child, and myself. It was killing me from the inside out, but from the outside in, it felt so good to wear the masks! I felt valid, powerful, and needed, but most of all it was a distraction from my deep pain.

I knew from the moment I heard of my husband's passing that there was a bigger purpose for his loss, and I've always strongly believed that everything happens for a reason. At that time though, I couldn't comprehend what that reason could be. He was my life and now he was gone. So I just shut down emotionally, and rather than hiding behind my husband, I became him. It was far less painful, or so I thought, than being me during this time.

After months of walking in his shoes, I began feeling the way he must have felt—overworked, depleted, repressed, and highly stressed. I missed spending time with my children. I missed cleaning my house. I missed having lunches with my girls. I missed my creative side gigs. I missed my husband. I missed my life!

I had gotten so caught up relentlessly pursuing what I had been programmed to believe was success and trying so hard to continue the legacy that we had collectively worked so hard to build, that I was killing myself. My spirit was dying, and I was essentially committing emotional suicide. It was time to cut my losses. It was time to redefine success. It was time to take off the masks. … Can you relate?

Your Turn!

Worksheets

Throughout this book I have provided contemplative questions and exercises that will assist you in your Awakening process.

Download your worksheets at ***www.MotherhoodsNotfor Punks.com/bonuses*** and revisit them as many times as you need to gain clarity.

1. Make a list of the masks that you wear.

_____

_____

_____

_____

_____

_____

2. What are these masks protecting you from?

_____

_____

_____

_____

_____

3. Under what code of honor or guiding principles (conscious or unconscious) have you been operating?

_____

_____

_____

_____

_____

_____

_____

_____

4. Define success.

_____

_____

_____

_____

_____

_____

_____

_____

Chapter 4

The Defining Moment

-4-

The Defining Moment

A pearl is a beautiful thing that is produced by an injured life. It is the tear that results from the injury of the oyster. The treasure of our being in this world is also produced by an injured life. If we had not been wounded, if we had not been injured, then we will not produce the pearl. - Stephan Hoeller

In all the years that we were together, for as long as I can remember, my husband and I had conversations about FREEDOM. Freedom to do and go and say what we wanted, when we wanted. Having the money and lifestyle to make anything a reality. Creating a legacy for our children that would change the lives of our family for generations. These were the things we talked about regularly. But I didn't realize at the time that there was another kind of freedom that my husband longed for—freedom from himself. Freedom from the expectations that he placed on himself. Freedom from the feelings of disappointment and unworthiness that he felt when he could not live up to those expectations. Freedom from the roles he found himself stuck in. Freedom from "The Masks."

I attempted to quench the emotional volcano bubbling inside me for a while with travel, shopping, partying, alcohol, sex, and other coping methods. I tried anything to mask my pain as I poured my time, energy, and resources into doing everything I could think of to make sure that my children were okay.

I sent them to grief camp, we read books about grief, I got them one-on-one NLP (neurolinguistic programming) therapy, we had weekly family circles to create space for healing conversations, they received Reiki healing, I arranged private retreats with a gestalt therapist to process grief and begin rebuilding our lives, and I sent them to teen development and leadership programs where they had the opportunity to connect with other teens that were moving through similar challenges.

I convinced myself that I didn't have time to deal with my own grief, and that I had to keep on pushing forward. But in July 2009, I could no longer hold back the hurt, tears, and the feelings of absolute despair, and they began to erupt uncontrollably.

Being everything to everyone, wearing the "Superwoman Mask," fed my ego. My identity had now shifted from being wrapped up in my family, to being wrapped up in how I was perceived in the world, how quickly I achieved the next level of success, what kind of leader I was, and how well I took care of everyone else. It felt good, people loved me, and I was thriving … but it came with a cost.

My spirit was dying. I was losing myself, and I was living a lie. One moment I was standing in the front of the room as a tenacious leader, motivating, inspiring, and training my team of over 100 financial agents, and the next minute I was on the bathroom floor curled up under the porcelain toilet heaving, crying, and praying to die. I was afraid. I felt trapped. I felt lost and alone, but no one knew. I didn't feel like I could share my pain because I was the one that everyone else went to for support, which created even more isolation and made it harder for me to consider taking off the masks.

For the first time in my life, I understood how someone could consider taking his or her own life. I didn't want to be here. I wanted out. But I had three—soon to be four—little kids depending on me,

Then in August 2009, after surviving a near fatal labor, birthing our healthy baby boy, and sinking deep into a depression, it became clear to me that I was not a victim and that no one was coming to save me. I had to save myself. I had to start putting ME first and create the time and space to deal with my grief. This would, of course, require me to reach out for help, which went against our family code of honor. But I was tired and I had nothing left to give, so I humbled myself to my pain. I laid down my masks, removed my cape, and searched out the people and the resources to guide me on my journey of Awakening Life.

In my marriage I had the freedom to BE me. I was the creative, free-spirited, free-loving butterfly and anal-retentive control freak of the relationship, and he was the overly ambitious, analytical, logical, structured one that let me think I was in control—although we both knew that I wasn't. We knew our roles in the relationship, and we stayed in our lanes.

Mine was a role I played well because it was authentically me. I was a stay-at-home mom (which I loved). I took incredible pride in caring for my husband and my kids, but I always had other projects, hobbies, and businesses that expressed my passions as well. His structure provided the framework for me to dabble in my purpose and use my unique gifts and talents without the risk of failure. It was the perfect arrangement.

It was easier and more comfortable for me to push him into the spotlight (which he loved) and support him in becoming successful than it was for me to step into the spotlight. I chose to "play small," partially because I knew that if I stepped out and pursued my passions on the level that I desired, it would negatively affect my family. He openly expressed his disapproval of any kind of fame or me being away from the family for long periods of time. But the biggest motivation for choosing to "play small" was fear—fear of success, fear of failure, fear of being seen, fear of being judged, and so on, and so on.

On my journey of self-discovery, I discovered that I had been hiding. I had consciously chosen to embrace the role of supporter because I was timid about my own personal power, self-conscious about my beauty, and afraid of what my personal success would do to the dynamics of my family. I consciously and successfully created this family as the antidote to my feelings of unworthiness. Who was I if I wasn't Alex's wife and Jorden, Ramses, Ajani, and now Taycuan's mom? Who was I without my role as the supportive wife and business partner? Who would I be if I weren't the person that everyone came to for advice, if our house wasn't the house that everyone came to for dinners or the holidays? What would everyone do without me? How would life around me go on? Pretty arrogant of me, huh? I know … but it was how I felt. My entire identity was wrapped up in my roles and the masks that I wore. I had completely lost sight of who I really was and what I wanted, and I didn't trust myself or the unique gifts that I had to offer the world. I knew that it was up to me to rewrite our story. So collectively, with my children, we began to create a new family code of honor based on something real.

Herein lay the defining moment that would change my life forever. It became evident to me that my husband had to be removed from my life in order for me to stop "dimming my light" and to risk being seen. My loss provided me an opportunity to remember who I am. It gave me the permission I needed to step into my greater purpose, redefine success, and completely deconstruct and rebuild my life based on a new value system.

My Fresh Start

In October 2010, I made the tough decision to take back control of my life by walking away from the financial business that my late husband and I spent twelve years building, and I began creating a life that was more authentic to me.

My decision was affirmed while I was on a spiritual retreat in Bali, Indonesia, in February 2011, where I was told by an elder shaman that I was a healer and that I would touch many lives.

"Our lives are shaped by the decisions we drape over the moments we can't escape." So instead of playing the victim, I chose to use the Wisdom gleaned from my experience to help others. My tragedy was the catalyst for my transformation.

Fast-forward six years, I'm now a thriving mom-preneur and author, a dynamic speaker that has graced the stages of Lisa Nichols, eWomen Network, and TedX, just to name a few ... and the creator of the Badass Bodacious Life Movement. My visionary work allows me to travel the world inspiring others through my Wisdom Teachings, inspired parenting techniques (including homeschool, mindfulness, and meditation), and my feminine model of entrepreneurship (you're reading my book!). I've successfully recreated my life and my parenting style, and I've helped hundreds of other women do the same.

What I discovered on my journey of re-creation is that life is a series of Awakenings: Awakening Self Esteem | Awakening Creativity | Awakening True Self.

As I walked through my journey of healing, I documented what worked for me, and from that I created the 6 Step Wisdom System that I have used for the last five years to help hundreds of women, CEO mom-preneurs, healers, and leaders. This process comes to life through my speaking, coaching programs, and retreats, but I will walk you through many of these nuggets in this book. It worked for me, and if you follow the system and create space to do the exercises, I know that it will work for you too.

It's your birthright to live with passion and purpose. Give yourself permission to awaken to the courage and confidence to live your best life.

Imagine that right NOW - in this very moment - you can set free the confidence and the courage to live your best life!

The Awakenings by Patrina Wisdom provides you exactly that! In three easy to understand guiding principles you'll discover ways to activate a true sense of direction and stand strong in your own power.

You'll find ways to release dis-empowering beliefs, and sabotaging actions. Free of persistent, limiting fears, that block the view of what's possible for you and your life,

You'll immediately gain access to more fulfilling relationships, clarity for empowered choices, sense of purpose, happiness, passion, and natural joy! But, best of all, you'll no longer let energy-draining expectations run your actions.

Instead you'll allow your own purpose, passion and true desires to be in control as you experience more of what you want in life, relationships and success.

Awakening Life Audio:
www.MotherhoodsNotforPunks.com/bonuses

Chapter 5

What I Learned

-5-

What I Learned

"Happiness cannot be obtained through levels of financial success or material things; happiness starts within. YOU are the common denominator of your life!"
-Patrina Wisdom

After countless coaching sessions, retreats, workshops, hypnosis, therapy, and hundreds of thousands of dollars of investment, I realized that it all came down to self-esteem, self-worth, mindset, and self-care. Everything we do and the way we live our lives are direct reflections of how we see ourselves. Oftentimes we want others to love us in ways that we are not willing to love ourselves. It is important to strengthen our self-esteem and practice self-love so that we can teach others how to love us.

Our self-worth is the foundation on which everything in our lives is built. How we show up in the world and for others is a direct reflection of our self-worth. Self-worth is something that we are born with and that no one can ever take away from us, but it is easy to lose sight of it—especially when you experience traumatic situations like loss and divorce. Our self-worth can also be affected when we spend time with people who don't value us. It is affected every time we are ridiculed, teased, put down about something, or compared to someone. In many cases our self-worth was shaken long before we even realized we had it. It's typically very early in our childhoods that we begin developing and wearing the masks.

A person who grew up being called "stupid" will start to believe that they are. As they grow older, they develop the need to prove that they are smart, so they may go and get multiple degrees. They show up in the world as someone who is driven, when in reality they are just covering up the fact that they believe or have been told that they are not smart. They are masking the real problem.

A person who was constantly called "selfish" as a child may grow up to be a caregiver—to the detriment of themselves—in order to mask the belief that they are selfish. A person who grew up getting little or no attention, had an absentee father, or was a product of divorce might suffer from feelings of not being enough. Well, if you see yourself as not enough, you may show up for others as someone who has to prove that you are. Your reaction to conflict may tend to be defensive because you are hurt, or you may become aggressive when someone challenges your being "enough."

In these moments it's important to take a pause. Pay attention to your self-talk or inner chatter. Work on resolving the real issue, and then make an empowered decision about what's next so that you don't continue reinforcing your old patterns. Many times our reactions to our deep emotional scars and self-worth issues are the reason that we are ineffective in relationships and business. They are the reasons we have misunderstandings and why we get so worked up and upset about the little things.

Worksheets

Throughout this book I have provided contemplative questions and exercises that will assist you in your Awakening process.

Download your worksheets at ***www.MotherhoodsNotfor Punks.com/bonuses*** and revisit them as many times as you need to gain clarity.

Answer the following questions:

1. On a scale of 1–10, how would you rate your self-esteem/ self-worth?

_____

_____

_____

_____

_____

_____

2. What are the top five challenges that you are experiencing in life, love, relationship, and career? Are these challenges persistent?

_____

_____

_____

_____

_____

_____

3. What do you think is at the root of all of these challenges? How can you shift this?

_____

_____

_____

_____

_____

_____

Chapter 6

The Heart of the Issue

-6-

The Heart of the Issue

"If you understand how the mind works, you're not afraid of it."
- Yoga Sutras by Patanjalese

As I began documenting my journey of healing, I began to notice repetitive patterns and voices that kept coming up, often stifling or preventing me from moving forward. So being the inquisitive Scorpio that I am, I began seeking out the deeper reasons for what might be driving my behavior and the behaviors of other women and moms. In my quest, I learned about the many different archetypes that exist. I was specifically interested in the ones that commonly show up for women.

The term "archetype" has its origins in ancient Greek. The root words are archein, which means "original or old," and typos, which means "pattern, model or type." The combined meaning is an "original pattern" from which all other similar persons, objects, or concepts are derived, copied, modeled, or emulated. The concept of archetypes implies that there are sources of health, healing, strength, and wisdom within the psyche that are accessible to us all.

I've heard of many different versions of archetypes over the last six years, but the ones that ring most true for me and my experience as a woman are the ones that I recently explored at my good friend Christina Dunbar's SHE Retreat in LA.

Feminine Archetypes:

Good Girl
Primal
Wise Woman
Magical Child

Our archetypes show up the loudest when we are up against our deepest fears or desires. When they show up in our lives, they are screaming for our attention.

Take a look at the more detailed explanations of each archetype below and see how they are showing up in your life. As you read through the archetypes, notice which ones make you feel empowered and which ones make you feel disempowered—notice, but don't judge.

Bringing awareness to these traits can help you to name them and call them out when they are present. Our goal is not to silence or kill any of our archetypes, but rather to integrate and embody all of them in the most empowering way possible.

1. The Good Girl

She is critical of herself and others
She never feels like she is good enough
She has challenges getting things done for fear of not being perfect
She is a people pleaser
She waits for permission
She doesn't allow herself to take up space
She has a fear of doing things wrong or going against the grain
She plays by the rules
She allows guilt to rule her

I've definitely struggled with these babies the most in my life. Growing up as an only child in a family rooted in Christianity, I was always being told by my parents and society to be a good little girl, speak when spoken to, and say I'm sorry; ladies are meant to be seen not heard, and so on and so forth. I'm sure you get the picture.

Society tells us to be polite, to think before we speak, to repress our sexuality, and not to make a fuss. Fuck that! Sorry? Not sorry anymore!

Women have been hushed and shamed for far too long. All of this programming that was meant to be for our own good has caused many of us to completely lose our voices. We have forgotten how to ask for what we want. Many of us are functioning and making decisions from a place of deep shame, blame, guilt, and regret rather than from feelings of wholeness and empowerment. We have been brainwashed to believe that what we want doesn't matter.

I learned early on in life that my job, as a woman, was to make sure that everyone around me was okay, that they were happy, and that it was more important to be loved than respected. This belief system was so engrained in me that when I was being molested by someone close to me and then date-raped by a boy I had a crush on for years, I couldn't for the life of me access my voice to yell "NO."

Worksheets

Throughout this book I have provided contemplative questions and exercises that will assist you in your Awakening process.

Download your worksheets at ***www.MotherhoodsNotfor Punks.com/bonuses*** and revisit them as many times as you need to gain clarity.

What has listening to this good-girl voice or archetype cost you?

Contemplative questions:

How does your good girl show up?

_____

_____

_____

_____

_____

_____

_____

How does she talk to you?

_____

_____

_____

_____

_____

_____

What does she say?

_____

_____

_____

_____

_____

What does your good girl need from you?

_____

_____

_____

_____

_____

What is your deeper truth?

Continue to write and explore in your journal about the times, experiences, and/or situations in which this good-girl archetype serves you and when she doesn't.

_____

_____

_____

_____

_____

_____

2. Primal Energy

Animal Essence

Present to everything around her
She is liberated/wild
Survival instinct/she seeks out prey and devours it
She is fierce/unstoppable
She is committed/focused
Her assertiveness makes her an action taker
She protects herself and her tribe
She hibernates to recharge
She allows herself to be raw or messy

Sacred Slut

Desire is natural/primal
Owns her sensuality/is sleek and seductive
Experiences pleasure through all of the primal senses
(taste, touch, smell, sound, sight)

Comfortable and confident in her body
In touch with her own divine feminine power
Owns her desires
Magnetizes her desires
Present/she savors every moment
Captivating/draws you in/can't take your eyes off of her

Primal energy is some of the most powerful energy that we can embrace and embody as women, but it's also the energy that most women run and hide from for fear of being shamed or ridiculed. It's our connection with self, our desires, our bodies, sensuality/sexuality, passion, and survival instinct. It's our inner huntress, and there are times when this inner huntress comes in handy.

What are the areas of your life where you could bring in more of your primal energy to achieve your desired result? Answer the following contemplative questions.

Contemplative questions:

In what areas of your life does your primal energy show up currently?

_____

_____

_____

_____

_____

_____

How does it feel to be in your primal energy?

_____

_____

_____

_____

_____

_____

What are the areas of your life where you could use more primal energy?

_____

_____

_____

_____

_____

_____

What are you afraid of? What judgments do you have (if any) of her?

_____

_____

_____

_____

_____

_____

Continue journaling about the role that primal energy plays in your life, and start playing with bringing this energy into different areas of your life to see what works.

_____

_____

_____

_____

_____

_____

3. Wise Woman

Matriarchal Energy

She is a student of life and her experiences have created her all knowing wisdom
She rests in her knowing
She doesn't judge or project her opinions or force her expectations onto others
She walks in her greatness/knows her power
She takes a stand for herself and others
She allows surrender vs. forcing
She embraces her feminine flow with grace
She embraces life in all its fullness

She is a master of self
She is loving/compassionate/nurturing to herself and others
She is connected with herself and spirit
She is connected to her unique gifts and purpose

The wise woman is what we all aspire to be, but it's important for you to understand that in order to embody the wise-woman energy, you must first embrace and integrate all the other archetypes. Don't use this archetype as an excuse not to be all the other things. Our wise woman is always present once we consciously choose to embody her. Answer the following contemplative questions to identify the areas of your life that could use more or less of your wise-woman energy.

Contemplative questions:

In what areas of your life does your wise-woman archetype show up currently?

_____

_____

_____

_____

_____

How does it feel when your wise woman is present?

_____

_____

_____

_____

_____

What does she say to you?

_____

_____

_____

_____

_____

What are the areas of your life where you could bring in more wise-woman energy?

_____

_____

_____

_____

_____

Is there an area of your life that could use less wise-woman energy?

_____

_____

_____

_____

_____

When you think of the wise woman, who can you use as a model? Why?

_____

_____

_____

_____

_____

4. Magical Child

Playful/lighthearted
Free
Open
Loving/forgiving/committed
Unafraid
Infinite possibilities/no limits
Imaginative/fantasy/inspired
Artistic/creative
Honest
Intimate
Innocent/pure
Connected with source, nature, senses, self
Community/inclusive

Flexible/goes with the flow
Out of the box
Alive/melts the hearts of others
Curious/explorative/in inquiry/discovering
Adventurous
Selfish/sacred selfishness
Gets her needs met

Oh, our magical child ... this is the energy that slowly disappears, the energy we disown when we get married, have children, own homes, and engage in careers—when we're "all growed up" as I like to say.

It's time to let her come out to play. Our Magical Child energy creates spaciousness and lightness. It feeds our soul on a deep level to be playful, curious, and open to receive all the love, support, and abundance that life has to offer. It's where our creativity and divinity lives. Can you give your magical child permission to come out and play more?

Contemplative questions:

How often do you allow your magical child to be fully expressed? How does it feel?

_____

_____

_____

_____

_____

How does your magical child affect others?

_____

_____

_____

_____

_____

In what areas of your life could you use more magical child energy? How can you honor her more?

_____

_____

_____

_____

How has denying your magical child affected your life?

_____

_____

_____

_____

_____

Chapter 7

Coming Out of Hiding

-7-

Coming out of Hiding

"Motherhood does not define who you are,
but your children are an external reflection of who
you've been."
- Patrina Wisdom

I have undergone an incredible transformation in my years as a parent. This transformation is reflected in my inner world and my outer world. I did my work! I dove into the deepest, darkest spaces within myself and faced my shadows. My soul has been liberated from the lies, expectations, and projections of others. I have found my voice—the gentle and the fierce. I am finally ready to be seen by my children and others in all my fullness. Every day I am discovering areas of my life that I have been (and sometimes I still am) hiding in, but I'm willing to be completely transparent about all of it and to be witnessed in my vulnerability.

It's been said that our romantic relationships are our biggest teacher, but I say motherhood is. You can't divorce your kids. It's an unconditional love and commitment that lasts forever. Motherhood will challenge you in ways that you never thought possible, and you will discover reservoirs of courage and compassion that you didn't know you had.

We must master ourselves before we can master parenting our children because they respond more to what we show them than what we tell them. Kids pick up on and respond to energy, so it's impossible to hide anything. They may not always know how to interpret or translate what they are seeing, but they feel it, and that can be dangerous because nine times out of ten they will assume that whatever you are feeling is because of something they have done. They tend to feel as if they have disappointed you or done something wrong; then they carry that guilt or feeling of being a disappointment into their lives.

So let's talk about visibility: your willingness to be seen by yourself, your children, in your career, and in your life.

What does it look like to embrace the Badass that you are as a woman and a mom and create your Badass Bodacious Life? Can you have it all when you do it all? I say YES! But you have to first get clear on the following things:

Who are you?

What is your life's purpose or goal?

What is your motherhood's purpose or goal?

What is your relationship's purpose or goal?

Stop focusing on your current reality and start focusing on what you want to create!

Many women and mothers don't take the time to think about what they want because they are focused on survival, on a spouse, or on making sure that the children are getting what they need. What they need is YOU! They need you to show up as ALL of who you are. By giving yourself permission to be fully self-expressed and by playing full-out in your life, you are giving your children unspoken permission to do the same.

Stop spending your time and energy coming up with the reasons why you can't do what you want to do.

Stop allowing fear or disappointment to keep you from creating. Creation is what life is all about. Your dreams don't have to be big; they just have to feel right for you. Your dream could be to spend quality time with your kids, to be the best wife you can be, to express yourself more artistically or sexually, or to take up a hobby. Maybe your dream is to be a high-profile entrepreneur or CEO, artist, or community leader. Whatever it is, it's the pursuit and being in action that makes you a Badass.

The magic of creation has nothing to do with getting what you want. It's about who you become in the process. As you explore and grow in your own self-mastery, you will begin to discover yourself as someone who can create ANYTHING that you desire, even when you have fooled yourself into thinking that you don't know how. You'll begin to realize that you have played an active role in creating your current reality, and that you have the power to change it.

Now, I won't sit here and say that the path of self-mastery and mindful mothering is easy because it's not. It's simple, but not easy. It requires a commitment from you to take full responsibility for all your thoughts, words, and actions. It involves an undying commitment to do and be better—a better person, a better mom, a better friend, and a contributing member of society. ("Better" in this context means being more conscious of how your thoughts and actions are directly affecting others, acknowledging the oneness of everything and everyone, and not contributing to feelings of separation.)

This requires practice. This will not happen overnight. It takes time to develop a heightened level of awareness and embodiment. You will come up against resistance. Your family, friends, and even your children will meet you with the most resistance because they won't understand who you are becoming. On a primal level they will want to protect you by trying to keep you in the box. They may wonder or question what your changes say about them. They may call you selfish, question your decisions, or think you've outright lost your mind. Don't resist the resistance. Lean into it because it's moving you closer to your goal of creating the life that you truly desire.

You can't change other people, but you can change yourself. As you change, everything around you will change. Be willing to let go and trust that everything is perfect. Don't settle for comfort; life is too short. Change is good. It brings us closer to who we really are. Be willing to be uncomfortable in the interest of growth. It takes the same amount of energy to create what you DON'T want as it does to create what you DO want. It's not enough to think, dream, and feel about what you want to do; you have to take action.

Liberate yourself. Embrace the feelings (and often discomfort) of expansiveness. You deserve to experience more joy, more fun, more aliveness than you are allowing into your life currently. Your experiences of success in life depend on your willingness to risk failure. Push your edges in relationships, push your edges in career, and push your edges around what you want to be in the world. Learn to appreciate the value of small changes. When you are actively engaged in making your dreams a reality, you don't have time to be comfortable or depressed.

Start focusing on HOW you want to create your Badass Bodacious Life, rather than focusing on all the reasons why you can't. Be clear on your why. The motivating "why" for everything I do is my children. I have a deep desire to show them what it looks like to live an extraordinary life despite life's pesky challenges. I want to leave a legacy that goes beyond money and material gain, a legacy of empowerment, freedom, fun, and Badassery!

How about you?

What do you want?

What is your deeper why?

What legacy do you want to leave?

What steps are you taking to make that happen?

I invite you to sit in inquiry around the areas of your life where you might be hiding, dimming your light, or not letting your voice be heard. How would your life change if you decided to show up fully in your life and play full-out? What would life look like if you could embrace your imperfection?

What are you hiding from? Are you hiding from yourself, from your children, from your greatness? What parts of yourself are you withholding from others? Are you dumbing down, dimming your light to make others feel comfortable, and/or playing it safe to avoid conflict or failure?

Take a moment to reflect on these questions and make some notes below. Dig deep.

_____

_____

_____

_____

_____

_____

_____

_____

_____

_____

_____

_____

_____

_____

_____

_____

_____

Now that you've given it some thought and identified what exactly it is you're hiding from, the big question is … will you walk through the door?

Will you risk change?

Will you do the work that's necessary to shift your perspective?

Are you willing to take this journey of self-exploration and self-mastery with me?

Will you trust yourself and me enough to let go of who you were in order to fully embody the powerful being that you ARE?

Will you make a new decision, or will you continue playing it safe?

You are the foundation of your life. Every thought, every emotion, and every decision you make creates your reality. You must build your life on a strong foundation. No one or nothing can complete you—not a relationship, your children, a job, nothing. You must be complete within yourself. You must work on becoming whole absent your roles, responsibilities, and significant relationships. You can manifest anything that you desire. The Universe/God/Spirit wants to provide for all your needs, but you must clearly place your order and then learn to let go and allow the Universe to do its work. You must also learn to have FAITH and believe that you are worthy to have all that your heart desires.

"Miracles can't happen when doubt is present."
-Patrina Wisdom

In order to create your "Badass Bodacious Life," you must learn to be intentional about every area of your life, including parenthood. You've got to get back in the driver's seat of your life, creating it instead of being reactionary and living by default. My intention is that the material covered in this book will support you living life in the offensive instead of living in a constant state of defense. I want to help you get out of your own way and clear the view of what's possible for you in your life.

I started my self-mastery journey around age twelve when I picked up my first personal-development book *You Can Heal Your Life* by Louise Hay. I believe that this is the reason that I have been able to move so gracefully and swiftly through all the challenges and traumas that I've experienced in my life. Personal development has been my lifeline, and I want the same for you. It's time to fill the cracks in your foundation and become the best woman and mom you can be for yourself, for your kids, and for humanity.

In the next section of this book, we will bring awareness to all your stinking thinking, learn how to eliminate the thoughts and beliefs that are not serving you, and begin installing new empowering beliefs and habits that will empower you to create a life you love!

We will do this by utilizing parts of my 6 Step Wisdom System that has been used to transform the lives of thousands of women around the world.

6 STEP WISDOM PROCESS

1. W – Who am I (true self-esteem, beliefs, permission)
2. I – Identify (blocks, core values, why)
3. S – Sacred self-care (eat, sleep, etc.; boundaries, rituals)
4. D – Declare (mission, purpose, vision statement/board)
5. O – Organize (scheduling, strategic plan, calling in)
6. M – Move (personal branding, execute with support) Take Action!

Our work together will be internal; therefore, the results will be intangible but very powerful! Remember that the process of self-mastery is an ongoing process and should become a part of your daily routine.

Take it seriously. Commit to it. You're worth it!

This beautiful meditation will assist you in strengthening feelings of self-love and remind you of who you really are. It is an offering from me to you that will encapsulate you in the nurturing energy of connection with the Goddess that you are and bring you back to the oneness of unconditional love.

Who You Are Meditation:
www.MotherhoodsNotforPunks.com/bonuses

Chapter 8

Awakening Self-Esteem

-8-

Awakening Self-Esteem

"Owning your story can be hard but not nearly as difficult as spending our lives running from it. Embracing our vulnerability is risky but not nearly as dangerous as giving up on love and belonging and joy-the experiences that make us the most vulnerable. Only when we are brave enough to explore the darkness will we discover the infinite power of light."
–Brené Brown

What I've found is that every time we experience a trauma it essentially chips away at our self-esteem. Every time you experience a heartbreak, loss, disappointment, failure, or moment of pivotal change, a part of you essentially dies and you have to develop a new part of yourself. If you don't have this awareness, then it's not likely that you will take time to heal from it. No one wants to admit that they have low self-esteem, but in fact, many of our challenges in life stem from it.

Case in point: As I explained earlier, My mom and dad split up when I was about four or five years old. My mom moved us from Las Vegas to New York to pursue a career, and not long after we moved, my dad got married. This marriage created a wedge in our relationship almost immediately because, for one reason or another, the new wife did not like me or want me in their life. She would feed me untruths about my dad and his feelings about my mother, and she would call me all kinds of bitches and treat me badly when my dad wasn't around. When I'd tell my dad about her bad behavior, he didn't believe me.

As a child, I felt abandoned by my father. I felt that he had chosen her over me, and it created feelings of unworthiness and not being "enough." This was my perception therefore making it very true and real for me.

The belief that I was not enough caused me to put myself in many compromising positions over the years in search of love and validation. I was unconsciously searching for someone to fill the void that my father had left, and my search resulted in a date rape and other negative outcomes.

So when my husband committed suicide, it triggered those feelings of abandonment, unworthiness, and not being enough, and I again started putting myself in compromising positions in an attempt to fill the void.

It wasn't until I stopped and allowed myself to sit in my pain that I recognized the pattern. I realized that I had been overcompensating in so many areas of my life for so many years in a desperate attempt to feel loved and validated and that this was directly related to the loss of my relationship with my dad at an early age.

For many people, abandonment issues manifest themselves by causing a person to isolate themselves, or shut people out of their lives. My fear of being hurt or abandoned caused me to do the opposite, making it less recognizable. I had a pattern of pushing myself onto people. I would go out of my way to be nice and accommodating in hopes that they would like me and want to keep me around. I was a permeable membrane, ready and willing to become whatever or whomever people needed me to be instead of being confident in who I was and what I had to offer people.

My husband had been the antidote to my pain for over twenty years. He provided me with a sense of security, and he helped me connect with my own worth. But now he was gone, and my scars were reopened. My self-esteem was shaken, and I felt abandoned once again. I was at a crossroads. I could either continue to ignore the real issues and search for someone new to fill that void, or I could learn to love myself and strengthen my self-esteem as an individual.

Does this sound familiar? Are you dependent on someone outside yourself, a title, a position at your job, a certain financial status, or acceptance in a certain social group to make you feel whole? This is just one example of how our past experiences can affect our self-esteem and our beliefs about ourselves.

As a child you truly believed that you could do or be anything that you wanted. You loved yourself, and you were naturally confident in the person that you were. When things went wrong, you were told that it wasn't your fault and you believed it. You would dance, and sing, and draw pictures, and create things. You believed in yourself and you weren't afraid of anything.

Well, what happened? What changed? Our experiences, our traumas, and people's judgments, opinions, and expectations of us happened. Over the years we have learned to suppress who we really are and what we really feel in the name of survival. I'm inviting you now to throw all that programming away and reconnect with who you really are. It's not as hard as it sounds or as far away as you might think, but you must first identify the traumas that chipped away at your self-esteem in the first place.

This is what worked for me:

1. Create a timeline of traumatic events. Include everything from your first move or death of a pet to divorce, rape, or passing of a loved one.

2. What beliefs have these events created in you? Have frequent moves made it difficult for you to connect with people? Has a cheating mate created the belief that all men lie and cheat? Were you teased in school, so now you think that you're fat, ugly, or stupid?

3. How have these events or beliefs affected your relationships and your decision making? Do you assume men won't be attracted to you? Do you shy away from opportunities to make friends or pass up opportunities to advance at work in fear of not being good enough?

4. Do these beliefs serve you in a positive way? No! Absolutely not.

We manifest the things that we put our energy into. So if you're always afraid of rejection, not being enough, afraid of being hurt, and so on—you will be!

In order to awaken self-esteem, we have to train ourselves to stop those negative emotions and fears dead in their tracks and shift our energy. Self-esteem does not develop overnight; it's an ongoing process. It's something you have to do or work on every single day. Healthy self-esteem is having an awareness of yourself, your thoughts, and your emotions and being willing to acknowledge and change what you don't like. It's a commitment to becoming your best self!

Healthy self-esteem will develop every time you keep a promise to yourself or someone else. It will develop as you shift from tearing others down to identifying and praising them for their gifts. It will develop when you lend a hand, a shoulder, or money when you don't have it to give. Awakening self-esteem is accomplished by giving yourself permission to stand strong in who you are and let your light shine.

Now that you have a more realistic understanding of what self-esteem looks like, let me give you some tips on how to start the process. Grab a pen and paper.

Do you have it? Okay, great!

Take some time to make a list of all the positive, beautiful things about yourself, about your body, about what you have to offer the world. Take your time creating this list. If you're having trouble thinking of things, ask close friends and family to tell you what they see, and then add those qualities and characteristics to the list.

Make a game out of it. Have fun with this exercise! This is a time to discover things about yourself that others already see, love, and appreciate—a celebration of the perfect being that you are, just the way you are. Spend a good amount of time on this exercise; you deserve it!

Once you have created your list, I encourage you to read it often … out loud and with conviction. When I was in my healing process, I would stand in front of the mirror in my bathroom, look myself in the eyes, and affirm at least one item a day from the list. It felt a bit awkward at first, but after a while it became fun, and more importantly, I started to believe what I was saying.

Awakening self-esteem is an ongoing process, but it can be done. They say that anything you do for thirty days in a row becomes a habit, so I suggest reviewing your list and affirming what you've written out loud for at least thirty days in a row.

Here are some other ways to awaken self-esteem:

Journal. Writing your feelings and experiences down gives you something to look back at in times of reflection. We write from the heart, so you will learn a lot about yourself and your motivations by reading it. Not only is it a great outlet, but it will also serve as a tool for healing. Journaling makes it easier to identify your emotional triggers and where they stem from so that you can choose to respond in a different way.

Example:

You're dating a man/woman, and you have texted them three times and gotten no response. Do you?

A. Assume they are blowing you off
B. Assume that they are with another woman/man
C. Assume they are busy and will get back to you later
D. Assume the phone died

Your answer will be a reflection of where you are with your self-esteem. If you chose answer C or D, you have healthy self-esteem as it relates to relationships. If you chose A or B, then you know that you have some work to do in that area.

Either way, it's okay because the awareness will allow you to address what's really going on inside you.

- Read positive, affirming books like this one (see suggested reading list in the back of the book).
- Participate in groups that focus on personal development.
- Reconnect with a higher power through church, meditation, or prayer.
- Surround yourself with a positive, affirming, supportive community of people.
- Start working out (physical fitness helps with energy levels and clarity).
- Cut out all negativity (negative people, television shows, music, etc.).
- Make time for self-care and personal retreats (unplug from all distractions and just do you).
- Sleep, read, draw, write, get a massage, or anything else that makes you feel good.

As your self-esteem improves, you will notice that life feels, smells, and looks so much better. You will open to more people and experiences. You will feel deeper connections with yourself, your kids, and all the other people in your life because you will no longer have to DO anything to be loved. Living in the authentic essence of Who You Are creates an opportunity for you to just BE.

Once you awaken your self-esteem, you will have more control over the outcomes in your life, you will feel more empowered, and you will no longer have use for a mask!

A great go to meditation to assist in bringing peace and healing into your consciousness.

This Violet Flame Meditation can be used to transmute and uplift your energy field. This powerful meditation will assist in dissolving lifetimes of unresolved, unhealed energies with love and light.

Violet Flame Meditation:
www.MotherhoodsNotforPunks.com/bonuses

Chapter 9

Awakening True Self

-9-

Awakening True Self

"Stop living by default and get back in the driver's seat of your life!"
- Patrina Wisdom

When was the last time you acknowledged your true self? Do you even know who you really are? I have found that many of us get so caught up in the roles that we play in life or the "masks" that we wear that we lose sight of who we are, and we end up settling or living by default.

So what does that mean? Well, we all know what it means to settle. "I'm not in love with him/her, but he/she is good to me," "We've been together for so long," "My biological clock is ticking," "I don't want to be alone," and/or "I hate my job, but it pays the bills."

If you hate your job, then why are you there? Why do you stay? There is probably someone else out there that would love to have your position, and there is a career that is more suited for you.

If you're not completely fulfilled in a relationship, why would you deprive yourself or your partner a chance at real happiness? Far too many of our decisions in life are driven by fear.

I bet there is someone out there that is a better fit for you and for your partner. I challenge you right now to open yourself up to new possibilities. I challenge you to start choosing faith over fear!

I started these Awakenings with Self-Esteem because it really is the root of all your problems. Your past experiences have shaped who you are. They have contributed to all your good and bad habits and choices and have shaped your perspective about your life. We usually refer to these past experiences as "issues" or "baggage" and we all have them, but we need to learn to move past them and make new choices. It's time to learn from our past experiences and use what we learned to create our future.

Question: If you were going to build a house, would you build it on a strong foundation or a weak one? A strong one, of course!

Well, let me ask you another question: How strong is the foundation you've built your house on? How solid is your self-esteem?

Do you know who you are? What you have to offer the world? How you need to be loved? How to give love without hurting or depriving yourself?

Have you ever stopped to think about how you show up in the world and how people perceive you? It's really important to connect with who you really are, what you really want and deserve, and how to give and receive love so that you show up in the world as a whole person. When your self-esteem is solid and strong, you will uphold your boundaries. You will feel worthy. You will have a greater vision for your life, and others will respond in awe to the beauty of seeing you step fully into your power.

No one is perfect. Like a house, things will always be shifting and changing. We will experience feelings and situations that may very well affect how we feel about ourselves, but we must learn to surrender and adjust. Having a strong foundation will help you bounce back quicker and easier because it will provide a point of reference for you to constantly re-assess what is truth and what are lies. With practice, you will begin to choose people and situations that affirm your truth, and you will create a whole new belief system that serves you. We all have imperfections, wounds, and negative beliefs about ourselves. What's important is that we acknowledge them and continually work on changing them.

Think of yourself like a house. You may have curbside appeal, and as you enter your house everything may even appear perfect and in place like you've got it all together. Then something happens. Someone enters your life and opens that one closet where you store all your issues and baggage, and everything comes tumbling out. Or they lean against what looks like a hairline crack in your wall, and your whole house comes tumbling down because when the crack happened, instead of dealing with and healing from it, you decided to paint over it in hopes that no one would notice. You told yourself that you would deal with that later.

What you didn't realize is that there are no quick fixes. What you didn't know is that life gets easier when we finally STOP and acknowledge and honor our own feelings and experiences instead of pasting on a fake smile and acting like everything is okay.

Self-esteem is strengthened every time that you show compassion for yourself, every time you choose to take care of yourself. I know that for all the caretakers out there this goes against everything you believe, but how long can you continue to give to others to the detriment of yourself? How will you care for others when you're not healthy? You must learn to fill your cup first and then serve from your overflow. Just like when you're riding on a plane, put your mask on first before assisting children and others.

When you put others above or before yourself, you get caught on the treadmill of being what everyone else needs you to be, when they need you to be it, and you lose sight of who YOU really are.

Every time you date someone that you know is not good for you, you chip away at your self-esteem. Every day that you go to a job that you hate and give away precious hours, days, and years of your life, it affects your self-esteem. Every time that you compromise yourself in any way, you are affirming to yourself that you are not worthy. You are devaluing yourself, and the sad part is that the more you do it, the easier it becomes and the less you recognize it. Your true self continues to shrink and fade to black, and then you wake up one day and don't even recognize the person you've become.

So how do we begin to change that? How do we go about reconnecting with our true self? The first step is what we've already done—work actively on strengthening your self-esteem. Once you remind yourself that you are worthy and that you have the power to create your reality, you can then begin to identify the habits and choices you've been making that are not serving you, and you can address them.

Ask yourself better questions, such as:

Am I afraid to be alone? Is it better to be happy alone, or miserable with someone else? What do I want my life to look like? What do I need to feel fulfilled in a relationship or a career? What do I have to offer the world?

I have found that people spend more time planning their day, a party, or a vacation than they do planning their lives. How difficult would it be for you to start giving yourself and your life the same time, consideration, attention, patience, and compassion that you give to a job/career, relationship, or your kids? In your career, if a person is not right for the job, you get rid of them. If you love what you do, then you go out of your way to please your boss and hold your position. In a relationship, you give all of yourself and bend over backwards to make your partner happy. With kids, you show so much compassion, and you protect and love them with everything that you have. Why don't you do the same for yourself?

What if you took the time to reconnect with your inner child, your true self? What if you stopped putting your own happiness and fulfillment on the back burner? What if you didn't need a partner, career, financial status, or title to make you feel whole? What if instead of depending on all of these external things for your happiness, it came from within you and those things just contributed to it?

How different would your life look if you believed you could and should have everything that you want—and if you believed that you deserve it? Because you do! Everyone is special and unique. Everyone deserves happiness. You're never going to find it if you continue to try to force things that don't fit. Figure out who you really are. Nurture your self-esteem, and once you strengthen it, protect it with everything you have.

Here is what worked for me. Grab your journal or some paper and a pen.

Now that you have completed the Awakening Self-Esteem exercise and have a list of all your wonderful qualities, gifts, and talents.

You are reading this book right now because when I made my list, I realized that I'm relatable, people like talking to me, I'm a good listener, I'm very positive, and I love to help people. I then took those and many other gifts and talents that were on my list and created a career for myself.

You've done your mirror work and affirmed yourself daily. You should be feeling pretty good about yourself and what you have to offer.

So let's get you started on Awakening Your True Self.

Make a list of all the ways that you have dishonored yourself in the past.

If you want people to respect you, you must respect yourself. If you want people to honor you, you must honor yourself. If you want to be loved, then you must learn to love yourself. Your relationships are indicative of the relationship that you have with yourself. Therefore the change begins with you.

Make a T-chart. Place all the disempowering beliefs that you have been holding onto that don't serve you on the left side, and on the right side list the new empowering beliefs that do serve you, the ones that are going to replace the disempowering ones.

Now note some of the things that you loved to do as a child. Maybe it was writing poetry, singing, drawing, or traveling. Then ask yourself, "When I was six years old, what did I want to be when I grew up?" Write it down.

What kind of friends did you have? How did you feel love? How freely did you give love?

Re-connect with the freedom of being you. Then what I'd like for you to do is take that list and decide how much of it you desire in your life now.

Finally, I'd like you to sit down and write out the vision you hold for your life from the perspective of your inner child. If money, time, and realism were not factors, what would be the vision that you hold for your life?

Really take your time with this exercise. Connect with it. Feel the emotion of having everything that you are writing down. Then when you're done, I'd like you to read it over and over again because this will be the blueprint that we will use to recreate your life of passion and purpose in the "Awakening Creativity" chapter of this book.

Bonus Exercise: Iyanla Vanzant says to write a love letter to yourself every day for thirty days and to mail it to yourself. Imagine how wonderful it would feel to get an unexpected love letter every single day affirming how magnificent you are. After thirty days of that, do you think that you would allow anybody to tell you otherwise? I say, create a vision for your life, read it over and over again, believe that it is possible for you, and put action to it. Before long, your life will be transformed.

Chapter 10

Awakening Sacred Self Care

-10-

Awakening Sacred Self Care

"Balance is not letting anyone love you less than you love yourself."
- Patrina Wisdom

Now that you have done some work around remembering who you are and reconnecting with your deepest desires, let's create space for expansion and possibility. It's time to reclaim your role as the STAR of your own life.

The practice of sacred self-care is a practice of creating a sacred relationship with yourself. It's about giving yourself permission to take up space, deepening your feelings of self-love, and creating wholeness within yourself, thereby setting the standard for how others should love you.

If you don't make time to be in relationship with yourself, why should anyone else?

As a mother, you take care of so many people and have so many moving parts to manage that it's easy to fall into the habit of putting your own needs on the back burner. Over time, the habit of self-less mothering can leave you feeling tired, depleted, depressed, and frustrated.

That is why I am an advocate of self-full mothering: filling your cup first; allowing yourself to overflow with self-love, energy, and inspiration; and then serving from your overflow. This allows you to show up for yourself and every person or project in your life as the highest and best version of yourself.

So what does a strong sacred self-care practice look like? How do you create this sense of wholeness? Good question.

Things to consider when creating your self-care practice are:

- Self-Love – The basics
- Self-Respect – Boundaries
- Self-Worth – Re-educate
- Self-Expression – What does it mean to you?

Worksheets

Throughout this book I have provided contemplative questions and exercises that will assist you in your Awakening process.

Download your worksheets at ***www.MotherhoodsNotfor Punks.com/bonuses*** and revisit them as many times as you need to gain clarity.

Self-Love – The Basics

Rate yourself on a scale of 1–10 (1 = needs improvement; 10 = impeccable)

Eating (frequency and quality of food) _____

Drinking an adequate amount of water daily _____

Participating in physical fitness (movement) _____

Getting enough sleep (6–8 hours) _____

Do you take time to get present and into your body before getting out of bed? _____

Do you take intentional pauses throughout the day to breathe? _____

How are your stress levels or tolerance? _____

Do you listen to your body and honor your emotions? _____

Results: Add your scores together.

If you scored 60 or above, you are taking some time for yourself and have a Sacred Self Care practice of some kind in place. You can now add things to your self care menu.

If you scored below 60, you should take some time to make a list of all of the things you desire to do and begin creating time for self care.

"Life isn't about finding yourself, it's about creating yourself."
– Unknown

What are you willing to sacrifice in order to make time for caring for yourself? You may have to get up earlier or stay up later to make time for these practices, but it's worth it.

Put some thought into how you can craft your self-care practice. Everyone's life and situations are different, but I'd love to offer some suggestions of things that have worked for me in hopes of sparking some creativity within you.

Find time to enjoy simple pleasures or stolen moments, as I like to call them. Make self-care a game, and celebrate each win. (Note: During your self-care time, commit to unplugging from all distractions—phones, computers, TV, etc.)

1. Quiet cups of coffee

This would ideally be done on a patio, balcony, or near water—whatever feels good for you.

2. Girlfriend time

This could be nights or weekends out, play parties at each other's homes, spa visits, or lunch dates.

3. Solo spa or pamper days

Spa days don't have to be extravagant or expensive. They can be done at home or at an establishment depending on your budget. Mine typically consist of a mixture of massage, facial, manicure, pedicure, steam, sauna, hot bath, hot tub, or just slathering bath salts and oils on my body in the shower. If you have a Korean spa or Thai massage place in your area, I highly recommend them. They are cost-effective and efficient.

4. Take a walk

I highly recommend walking at the beach, lake, a park, or just around your neighborhood.

5. Solo picnic in the park or your backyard

Make yourself a picnic lunch containing your favorite foods or snack and enjoy a quiet, intentional lunch alone. Savor each bite. Enjoy your surroundings.

6. Snuggle up with a good book and read (How long has it been since you've done that?)

Sit in your favorite chair, grab a snuggly throw blanket, and read. This is simple and nurturing to your soul.

4. Take a nap

How often does your body tell you that it needs to rest and you just ignore it? Give yourself permission to steal naps here and there. Something as short as a twenty-minute nap can revitalize your energy and clear your mind so that you can complete tasks in a more efficient way.

5. Date nights with yourself

Take yourself out for a drink or a meal or to an art gallery or museum. Your social life does not need to be dependent on anyone else. Once you strengthen your relationship with yourself, you can be anywhere (with or without anyone) and have fun.

6. Morning rituals

This can consist of a number of things, but my morning ritual consists of waking up when my body is ready (if that luxury is available to you), taking some time to breathe and get into my body, gently rolling out of bed to tend to my personal hygiene, and doing a little yoga movement to loosen the rickety bits.

Once I am dressed and ready for the day, I set my intention for the day (what I want to experience, how I want to feel), and I take five to ten minutes of meditation (in my sacred meditation space). Then I pull an oracle or tarot card from one of my decks as a way to connect with my inner guidance.

(Note: This is all possible because I have trained my children to knock before entering my room, and I have trained them to honor my space and morning practice.)

You may need to set a clock and wake up a bit earlier to make time for your morning ritual, but I guarantee that if you commit to this practice, your days will be more joyful and you will get more done.

7. Evening Rituals

Evening rituals create space for quieting your mind and settling your body so that you can get a good night's sleep. By the evenings though, I am usually pretty beat, so my evening ritual is simply to take a shower and wash the energy of the day off me. I then review my calendar and make preparations for the next day.

Once that is done, I take a few moments to breathe and reflect on the happenings of the day before quieting my mind and going to bed. Sometimes I need to write in my journal or do some meditation to quiet my mind before bed. Find what works for you.

Self-Respect – Boundaries

Your outer world is a reflection of your inner world. The state of your house, car, clothing, relationships, and finances reflect back to you the areas of yourself and your life that need attention. Your circumstances and experiences are always speaking to you, so listen closely. What are they telling you?

Create Your Sacred Space

Every woman should have a space in her home that is just for her. Men do it all the time (the man cave). We could actually learn a lot from men. Men are brilliant at self-care, boundaries, and creating their sacred spaces.

When creating your sacred space, consider all your senses (taste, touch, smell, sound, and sight). It should be a space that you desire to be in, one that makes you feel really good.

My sacred space is my bedroom (but I'm a single gal). Yours may be a corner in your room, your bathroom, or a spot in the backyard or on your patio. It could be as simple as setting up a little altar table and placing a few of your favorite things on it. Find a space that works for you.

Once you have created your sacred space, you'll need to train your kids and partner to respect it. This may call for an explanation of why Mommy needs her own sacred space and how having your time benefits them. It's worth taking the time to explain.

Self-Worth – Re-educate

What are five expectations you have of yourself?

_____

_____

_____

_____

What are five expectations that other people have of you that you do not resonate with and want to free yourself from?

_____

_____

_____

_____

_____

What are five expectations that society has of you that you do not resonate with and want to free yourself from?

_____

_____

_____

_____

_____

Write down all the judgments that you have around each of these expectations. What does not living up to these expectations mean to you or make you?

_____

_____

_____

_____

Can you see how many of your choices and actions are not being led by your true desires?

A great deal of your behavior is based on WHAT YOU THINK OTHERS THINK OF YOU. We behave in a manner that is consistent with what we believe. So if you believe that others think a certain way about you, then you will tend to behave in a way that supports the belief.

Choosing to let go of all the unrealistic expectations that you have of yourself and the expectations that you think others have of you, along with choosing to let go of your fears, will help you take back control of your life. It will help you to identify and utilize your unique gifts, talents, and passions, and it will bring tremendous value to your life, your family's life, and to the world.

External events and circumstances can never hold you back. Only you can hold you back. YOUR thoughts, YOUR habits, YOUR mindset. It takes courage to look at your life and identify what isn't working. It takes courage to admit to yourself that something must change ... or to discover that *you* may be what needs to change.

Taking time for self-care will create space to notice what's present for you. Ask yourself questions and answer from a place of truth. Release the need for others to complete you. You were born whole and complete. Everyone and everything else in your life is just a complement to your life.

Self-Expression – What does it mean to you?

My Badass Bodacious idea of full self-expression means integrating ALL parts of yourself—owning your worth, finding your voice, and being unapologetic about who you are.

Authentic self-expression can act as a filter for you in your life. When you are being all of yourself, you will attract the people into your life that love who you are, and the people who are not in alignment will fall off. This is how we create an unconditionally loving community and the feeling of heaven on Earth.

There are many ways to express yourself. You can do it through your communication style. You can do it through your body language. You can do it through art, dance, poetry, song, photography, and many other ways. Find your thing.

Ask yourself:

What parts of myself am I currently repressing (e.g., artistic, playful, sexual, intellectual)?

_____

_____

_____

_____

_____

What is blocking me from expressing these parts of myself? What am I afraid of?

_____

_____

_____

_____

What are the consequences or outcomes I am experiencing by repressing these parts of myself?

_____

_____

_____

_____

_____

How would it feel if I gave myself permission to let her come out and play?

_____

_____

_____

_____

_____

What message would I send to my children if I did so?

_____

_____

_____

_____

_____

It's time to come out of hiding. Stop dimming your light to make others feel comfortable. Stop taking the backseat. Stop questioning. Stop making life harder than it has to be. Stop getting in your own way.

You're not just a mom. You're a Goddess! You are powerful beyond belief! You are Mother Earth! You give life! You are a creator! You are a leader! You are a visionary! Your presence shifts energy and transforms lives! You are a contribution with Who You Be in the world!

Chapter 11

Awakening Creativity

-11-

Awakening Creativity

*"There is nothing more fulfilling than saying YES
to something that you were unsure how to do,
figuring it out along the way, and succeeding at
doing it! Step outside the box and open the door
for new opportunities."*
– Patrina Wisdom

My definition of creativity is making something out of
nothing. Whether it be in business, finance, relationship, or
even your approach to parenthood, it is up to you to use your
creativity to manifest positive results.

When I lost my husband, I realized that creativity is happening all the time. My husband was the sole financial support for our family, and in his absence I was left to take the reins. Funny thing is, when you have multiple children, a good-sized home, luxury cars, and a "lifestyle" that you've become accustomed to, there aren't many jobs that pay enough to support it, and even if there were, I wouldn't qualify. I don't have many hard skills, nor do I have a degree in anything. In short, it would cost me more to get a job than it would to create a career for myself. Entrepreneurship allows for such creativity. I decided to use my natural talents and gifts to create a business model for myself that would fit into the parameters of my life.

Awakening Creativity is knowing that infinite possibilities exist and that they can exist for you. It's acting on inspired thought because you recognize that it might just be God showing you the way. Awakening Creativity involves your willingness to hear, surrender, and put action behind your desires. It's not just positive thinking; it's knowing that things have to work out for you—almost like a sense of entitlement.

We have all been given grace from God, and grace by definition is God's unmerited favor. It's our free gift from God. We wouldn't get a free gift from a department store and not use it, so why don't we acknowledge and utilize our grace from God? We all talk about faith, but how many of us are actually exercising it?

Know what you want. Believe that you can have it. Put action behind it, and have faith that God or the universe will deliver.

Prayer = Asking (from your mouth to God's ear)

Meditation = Receiving (bringing God's energy in and being open to receive)

Action = Taking (the necessary steps to get what you're asking for)

These ingredients = Manifestation of your desires!

Awakening Creativity means learning to be flexible. It means practicing trust and patience, knowing that things will always work out in God's time and according to his plan, not yours. When faced with challenges, don't try so hard to remove them; learn to move around them, like the river around the river rocks.

Try new things to produce new and different results. What do you have to lose? Worst-case scenario? Something changes … for the better.

Awakening Creativity in Business

We are forced to be creative in all areas of our life as it relates to problem solving. The better you get at being creative, the easier your life will become. When coming up with solutions to problems—whether they are in business, relationship, or anything else—it's important to know what the desired outcome looks like. So if we are talking about a business, you need to have a vision of what the business looks like and then figure out what steps need to be taken to make it happen. But first, you need to really evaluate whether or not you want to be an employee, self-employed, a business owner, or investor.

If you've read Robert Kiyosaki's *Cashflow Quadrant*, then you know what I'm talking about, but if you haven't, here is a quick review.

Employee: work for an employer, paid a salary for your time, safe, presumed secure, benefits

Self-Employed: independent, be your own boss, set your own pricing (value for money), own your job, only twenty-four hours in a day to work—you don't work, you don't get paid, and your income is dependent on other people.

Business Owner: own a system, surround yourself with smart people, delegate, lead people

Investor: your money makes money; convert your money to wealth.

Which one are you?
Which do you want to be?
Figure out which option lines up with the life you desire.

Ask yourself good explorative questions like:

1. What are your Top 5 Core Values? (You'll want to build your life and career around these values so that you're creating a life that's aligned with who you are.)

2. What impact do you wish to make on the world?

3. What kind of lifestyle do you desire?

4. How much money do you need to support your desired lifestyle?

5. What can you create that people need?

6. What service can you provide that people will joyfully pay for?

Wherever you are and wherever you decide you want to create is perfect. My goal is just to make you aware of where you are now and to present options. The key to creating a Badass Bodacious Life is exercising choice.

You don't have to recreate the wheel. You can take a business model that already exists and put your own personal spin on it. Pinpoint what or how your business will be different, and don't be afraid to borrow knowledge. Read related books, search the Internet, or ask people that have already been successful in the field you're looking to tackle.

Then test it out. No one is saying you have to be fully committed from the start. There are plenty of people out there working full-time jobs and building full-time businesses part-time. So many times we get caught up thinking things would only be better "if" ... and instead of testing something out, we either jump in with eyes wide shut or we stand paralyzed in fear. I'm offering you the opportunity to have your cake and eat it too, keep your security, and try something new.

Some Other Ways to Awaken Creativity

Maybe you have to be creative with your clothes because things don't fit the way they used to, or you have to be creative in the kitchen because you don't feel like going or can't afford to go food shopping.

I know that I myself have had to use my creativity when reprimanding my children. Kids are smarter and savvier than they used to be, and traditional punishments don't always work.

I was having incredible challenges with the school system because my kids have the nerve to have minds of their own and question authority. I have raised them to be confident leaders, stay curious, and question everything. That didn't go over too well in school, so I pulled my kids out and started homeschooling them. I didn't want my kids to be forced into a box that has taken me years and hundreds of thousands of dollars to break out of.

Was it a sacrifice? Yes!

Was I scared and insecure about whether or not I was making the right decision? Yes!

Did the people around me think I was nuts? Yes!

But I knew that I had to use my creativity in order to get my kids' needs met.

It turns out that homeschooling has been a huge gift. My kids are excelling academically, I've been able to incorporate meditation and yoga into our homeschool routine, and the flexibility of homeschooling has made it easier for me to conduct business from anywhere in the world, which supports my number one core value ... FREEDOM!

The lesson here is:

Learn to create a win-win situation. Anything you want or want to do is possible if you'll just use your creativity. Create a win-win for the person you need something from. Get in the habit of thinking value for money. If you don't have money, what value do you bring? Do you have a gift or talent that people will pay for, or something to give in exchange for what you're asking?

Here are some examples:

- I want to take a cruise, you want to fill your cruise ship. If I can get fifteen to twenty people to book a cruise, will you give me mine for free?
- Recently I wanted to do private yoga classes, but I didn't want to go to a public yoga studio. The schedule didn't fit my needs, and I didn't want to pay for private instruction. Instead, I negotiated a deal where if I could get four to six other people to attend at $20 each, at a time and place of my

choice, my class would be free.

Whether it's in business, relationship, or any other situation, there are five questions you want to ask yourself when attempting to solve any problem.

1. What have I done in the past?
2. What do I have to offer?
3. What do I need?
4. What do they need?
5. How can we create a win-win?

Stop asking *why*, and start asking *what*? It opens up possibilities for you, and it keeps energy flowing in a more creative, positive way. Remember that anything is possible if you focus on the big picture. Start the race with the vision of your victory in mind. All you need is a little confidence—and a lot of courage—to Awaken Your Creativity.

Chapter 12

Self-Mastery

-12-

Self-Mastery

*"Success is not a destination.
It's a by-product of a life built on who you are and
how you want to live your life."*
– Patrina Wisdom

Don't allow your dreams to die because you're a parent. Juggling motherhood and a career or entrepreneurship is a balancing act. It requires pre-planning, time-management skills, strong boundaries, and the ability to ask for and receive help, but it can be done successfully.

Far too many women and mothers spend too much time thinking about what they want to do and not enough time in action. They expend their time and energy coming up with the reasons why they can't do what they want to do, or they allow fear or disappointment to keep them from moving forward. It's time to get unstuck! You can't change other people, but you can change and become the master of yourself. As you change, everything around you will change.

Stuck is an emotional and psychological experience; it's not real.

Different kinds of STUCKNESS:

- A feeling (abandonment, not enough)
- Victimization—believing that the circumstances or events are bigger and more powerful than you
- Blame, shame, guilt, or regret
- Thoughts, limitations, or stories based on wishful thinking or wanting everything at once
- Behaviors (procrastination, perfectionism, over-serving); feeling unmotivated, scattered, unorganized, overwhelmed, and/or tired
- FEAR—fear of success, fear of failure; feel the fear and do it anyway.

Take baby steps every day toward making your goals and dreams a reality. Be patient. Remember that there is no real end goal. When you're living life to the fullest, you will be dreaming bigger, raising your mindset, expanding your vision of what's possible, and creating constantly.

Each moment that you experience is just a blip on the map of the journey of your life. Keep your focus on the bigger picture. Don't get wrapped up in rejection, disappointment, and setbacks because they are temporary. Don't use financial hardship, kids, or anything else as an excuse for not pursuing your dreams. Believe, trust, and be patient.

Short-term decisions have long-term consequences. Don't give power to the mistakes of the past. Create your new reality.

> *"Change your focus; change your lens.*
> *Move from victim to victor."*
> — Patrina Wisdom

Thoughts create your beliefs and paradigms. They create the filters through which you see your world. Your beliefs then determine the actions that you will or will not take. Your actions (or lack thereof) are responsible for the results that you have been getting in your life. Decide what you want. If you don't write your story, your disempowering beliefs and experiences will.

So how do you begin to write your own story? Again, take baby steps.

Start by clarifying and stating your intentions. What do you want to create in the next ninety days? How do you want to feel? Then take some time to sit down and consciously create your 90-Day Manifesto. This is a very detailed account of what you want to create that is written in present tense (as if it's already happening).

To get started, use the date that you're writing the manifesto as the specific date (ninety days out) by which you want to manifest your desires. Write out everything that you want in present tense, and be sure to include everything that you want to have, experience, and feel in the areas of health, wealth, family, relationship, career, home, spirituality, and any other areas that are important to you. Be very specific. Write everything out in detail as if it has already happened.

Here is an example of how to start this process:

I can't believe it's October 11, 2015, and I have met and settled into a relationship with the love of my life. From the time I met him, I knew that he was something special, but I decided to sit back and allow him to court me. He chose me, and it feels wonderful!

Can you see how writing out the experience of having what you desire can assist you with magnetizing them? It really is magic … and you hold the magic wand.

Once you have explored and written out in detail what it is that you want to create, it's time to ask yourself, "Who do I need to become in order to align myself with what I am asking for?" Are there some belief systems, old disempowering stories, or habits that you need to let go of?

Be willing to acknowledge that you may not always know what's best for you. Something better than you could ever imagine may be waiting for you once you grow into the person who is ready and willing to receive it. Self-mastery is about making choices and having the discipline to do the things that will put you in alignment with your goals. It requires a new way of thinking and being.

Stephen R. Covey says in his book *The 7 Habits of Highly Effective People* that:

Knowledge is the theoretical paradigm—the *what* to do and the *why*.

Skill is the *how* to do it.

Desire is the motivation—the *want* to do it.

In order to make something a habit in our lives, we have to have all three.

Self-mastery invites you to move from dependence (you take care of me, you didn't come through for me, I blame you), to independence (I can do it, I am responsible, I can choose), to interdependence (we can do it, we can collaborate and co-create together).

In order to move from a mindset of ME to a mindset of WE, you must shift from thinking and functioning from a place of scarcity and fear (there's not enough for me, what if it doesn't work) to thinking and functioning from a place of abundance (there is more than enough for me, things always work out for me).

Never make decisions when you're in a scarcity mindset. These are times when you are stressed or frustrated, financially or emotionally depleted. You will get much better results and realize the magic of your manifestation powers when you make decisions from a place of excitement, inspiration, and an abundance mindset.

Goal Setting

I am a huge fan of hard-core goal setting with milestones and timelines; however, I am not a fan of beating yourself up when you don't achieve the goals. Setting goals gives you a clear picture of what you want to create and a deadline for accomplishing that, but I have learned that it is important to release all expectations and attachment to HOW things show up (the outcomes). Things don't always present themselves in the way that you would expect, but know and trust that whatever shows up is always for your highest and best.

When setting goals, remember to consider all areas of your life.

- Physical – exercise, eating, sleeping, movement, stress management
- Mental – reading, continuing education, visualizing, planning, writing
- Emotional – sacred self-care, communication, getting your needs met in your relationships with yourself and others
- Spiritual – reconnecting with your core, your center (presence), your core values

The words that come out of your mouth coupled with the actions you take daily and your interactions with others should be in line with your core values and desired outcomes. Pay attention and course correct along the way.

"Walk your talk so you don't have to talk so much."
– Patrina Wisdom

Time Management

People make time for the things that they want to do. Organizing and executing around your priorities will help you achieve this. Be committed enough to your goals to create space for them, despite all the other obligations and responsibilities that you have to tend to.

Learn to delegate through time management and/or farming out tasks and responsibilities to other people (your kids, for example). There is no need to do it all. People love to feel a part of something. Engaging others in your dream will provide support and the accountability needed to get things done.

Schedule Everything

Don't overdo it. Plan out your time in such a way that everything gets done, in a way that leaves you feeling successful and fulfilled rather than tired and depleted. Believe it or not, not everything has to get done today. Take some pressure off yourself whenever possible.

1. Schedule time for sacred self-care daily or weekly (review chapter 10).
2. Schedule playtime for yourself (Mommy play dates).
3. Plan a weekly date night (whether you're single or in a relationship).
4. Plan for family days (take turns choosing activities and outings).
5. Plan for a healthy amount of sleep (six to eight hours per night).
6. Schedule time to plan meals each week (maybe even prep them and have them ready to go).
7. Whether you are an entrepreneur or work a nine-to-five job, put your business hours in your calendar.
8. Schedule a planning day to organize and review your calendar, pre-plan meals, set weekly intentions, prioritize projects to focus on, create contact lists, do laundry, etc.).

In order to have it all, you must find ways to be more efficient.

Delegate

Now, just so you know, I am a recovered control freak, so this is never easy for me to do. My ego had me tricked into believing that things would be done right only if I did them. What a load of bullshit. There are so many people out there that are more qualified to do certain tasks than I am. I just had to exercise my trust muscle, let go of expectations of perfection, and open myself to being supported.

How to get started:

1. Make a list of everything that has to be done in your home and in your business.

2. Decide which of the tasks you want or feel that you are best qualified to do.

3. Make a "possibilities list"—people that you may be able to assign tasks to (be specific about frequency and the time frames around your needs).

4. Give your kids more responsibilities around the house. Train them on how you want things done and attach an incentive of some kind. (Remember to praise them and affirm to them what a great job they are doing and how much their collaboration means to you.)

5. Buy back some time by investing in house help (housekeeper, nanny, tutor, chef, or order ready-made healthy meals).

6. Hire a virtual or personal assistant.

Do whatever it takes to create more ease and grace in your life. If you don't have the money to pay help, find ways to create a win-win. Get creative.

This may sound like a lot of work initially, but once you create these new habits, put strong systems in place, and commit to staying focused on the things you want to create for your life, the easier things get. Efficiency, magic, and creation become your new normal and your day-to-day life becomes a hell of a lot more fun.

Find Your Tribe

Surround yourself with positive and supportive people; do not engage in negative conversations or put yourself in low-frequency situations. Your reality is shaped by the influence of the 5 percent of the people you spend the most time with.

If you spend time with people who complain all the time, you will complain. If you are around people with small minds and victim mentalities, you will become so. If you are around people who question your abilities and downplay your dreams, you will do the same.

Dream out loud! Dream emotionally, and then apply strategy to those dreams. Share your dream with others. Ask for help. Be part of a Mastermind group, a dedicated time and space for a group of people to exchange ideas, brainstorm next steps, collaborate on projects, support each other, and tap into a collective energy field to uplift, up-level, and increase visibility.

Mentorship and tribe are important parts of goal achievement.

We all need a safe place to land: a person or a group of people we can talk to about anything without judgment or suggestions from them, someone to hold space while we share and who will honor our experience.

Be careful with whom you share your dreams and experiences. Share only with people that you love, trust, and/or admire; people who have been where you are going or who are doing or have what you desire.

Examples:

Get business guidance from someone who has a successful business or has built a successful business.

Get marriage advice from someone who has a happy marriage.

Get dating advice from someone who is actively dating.

Get parenting advice from moms that you admire.

Seek out mentors, coaches, and Mastermind or community groups that stand for personal and business development and transformation, hold yourself accountable to your greatness in a loving and compassionate way, create a safe space for you to unleash all the light and dark aspects of life that you are dealing with, and support without judgment. You're going to lose belief at one time or another on your journey. Your tribe of supporters will be the ones who will help you through those times. Borrow their belief in you and your dreams.

It's not enough to think, dream, and feel about what you want to do; you have to take action. Appreciate the value of small changes. Don't settle for comfort; life is too short. Be willing to be uncomfortable in the interest of growth and fulfillment. Your success in life depends on your willingness to experience and overcome failure.

"Life is what happens when you step outside of your comfort zone."
– Unknown

10 Step Goal Achievement [Cheat Sheet]

Connect with your bigger why. What's your leverage, motivation, or why must you achieve this goal?

1. What will not achieving this goal cost you?
2. What do you have to lose?

3. Prioritize your goals: immediate, short- and long-term goals.

4. Set SMART goals: Specific, Measurable, Achievable, Realistic, Time limited

5. Check in with yourself to make sure that your natural gifts and talents, true interests, purpose, core values, and passions are in line with your goals.

6. Create a compelling vision (90-Day Manifesto): a big-picture vision of what you want and why you want it.

7. Determine your goals and create action steps to support them.

8. Set or identify milestones and celebrate every success (builds confidence and esteem).

9. Overcome challenges along the way with the support of your tribe members.

10. Be more courageous, achieve more, step fully into your greatness, and feel more successful overall!

Chapter 13

Mommy Archetypes: What kind of mother are you?

-13-

Mommy Archetypes:
What kind of mother are you?

*"Motherhood will bring up all your shit.
Don't repeat the patterns of your past. Don't
overcompensate or use your kids to fill the void.
Write a new story."*
– Patrina Wisdom

When I started writing this book, I had no plans to focus it on motherhood. My intention was to share my journey, inspire women, and show that you can overcome any challenge and create a great life. But as I began writing, it became clear that it was all about the journey of motherhood.

The motivation for everything I do is my children. Motherhood has changed the way I looked at the world, and my children have inspired me to do and be more. Motherhood is the spiritual journey that has made me who I am today.

Motherhood challenges us to meet ourselves with love, patience, compassion, and mercy so that we can then do the same for our children. It's about acknowledging that our children are a direct reflection of all that we are. What you love about them is in you. What makes you crazy about them is in you.

What is your motherhood style?

Is your motherhood style speaking to you?

We all want our children to love, respect, and admire us, but how do we do that?

There are some parents that go the route of the traditionalists whereby they do things exactly the way their parents did it because it worked for them or because "I came out okay." Others enter into parenthood with the idea of wanting to do better than their parents did with them. But often the desire to do things differently causes them to overcompensate in many ways, which can in turn create a sense of entitlement in their kids or patterns of codependence.

As a Scorpio, I am a natural investigator. I have a tendency to notice everything because I watch, and I listen intently. I have a special gift for identifying patterns and inconsistencies, and I have a knack for solving problems.

Over the years I've witnessed quite a few motherhood styles, and I noticed some trends and patterns that I'd like to share with you. My hope is that this information will help you identify your parenting style and the impression that you may be making on your kids.

The following archetypes are not scientifically proven. These are archetypes that I have developed from years of observation and working with clients. It is just information. As you read through the archetypes, notice what resonates with you and what doesn't and then decide which traits or ways of being are serving you, and where you have room for improvement.

Archetypes:

1. Perfectionist/OCD Mom
2. Free-Spirited/Hippie Mom
3. People-Pleaser Mom
4. Trophy Mom
5. Mindful Mom

1. Perfectionist/OCD Mom

"Mask of Perfection" or "Superwoman Mask"

She is externally motivated
She works hard to maintain a pretty picture for the outside world
She puts pressure on herself and her kids to be perfect
She is often fanatical about keeping a meticulous, model-like home and/or personal presentation
Her children's individual needs or gifts are not acknowledged or nurtured
She is very systematic/plays by the rules

Chores and should-do's take up time that could be spent with her children

Praise is given only upon the fulfillment of her standard of success

She judges everything and everyone/very critical/nothing is ever good enough for her

She likes to do everything on her own/never asks for help because she feels it won't be done correctly unless she does it

She places unrealistic expectations on herself and on the children

She does not acknowledge or express her emotions in front of her kids

Her kids in turn feel like it's not okay to show emotion

She secretly feels isolated and unsupported

She has a deep fear of losing everything

Everything is black or white/either-or/uncompromising

Her identity is wrapped up in achievements and success

She won't take many risks herself, but will encourage her kids to do so

She tries to keep up with or surpass the Joneses

She often feels unworthy or insecure

She functions from a place of pushing and forcing

She is typically not receptive to help or support; has too much pride

2. Free-Spirited/Hippie Mom

She respects nature, spirituality, and humanity

She feels liberated/free spirit

She lives in flow/less structured

She is health conscious/holistic

She believes that life and our bodies speak to us

She is community-minded

She is uninhibited/embraces nakedness (physically and emotionally)

She is open and accepting

She is unattached to the material world; minimalist
She is inclusive; child is involved in most aspects of her
life
Her child's spirit is nurtured
Her child feels seen, honored, loved, and accepted as they
are
Her child is encouraged to use their voice
She creates an experiential environment for her family
She is energetically connected with her child
She is very hands-on

3. People-Pleaser Mom

"Caretaker Mask" or "Savior Mask"

She is self-sacrificing
She is often tired and overworked
She embraces the role of the martyr/plays the victim
She has not established strong boundaries
Her kids often run the home/lack discipline because she
wants them to like her
She is easily distracted by what others need/can be thrown
off course
She wants people to like her
She tends to be an over giver/often takes care of others to
the detriment of herself
She doesn't take pride in her appearance and lacks in the
area of self-care
She is overwhelmed and stressed out most of the time
She has lost her voice/stays
She is indoctrinated/plays by the rules
She lives in survival mode
She denies herself pleasure
She rarely asks for help
She does not want to outshine her kids

4. Trophy Mom

"Mask of Perfection" or "Superwoman Mask"

She is externally motivated
She wears the mask of perfection
She struggles with trying to be a perfect partner and
mother; to please husband, family, or other role
She often feels disconnected from her kids
She may have house help (housekeeper, nannies), not
because she needs them but because she can
She overcompensates her kids with things
She puts on a show for others
She hides her pain
She is success driven/materialistic/has something to prove
She is always in competition, comparison, and judgment of
others and sometimes with her own children
She is assertive
She is critical of herself and others/always looking for what
what's wrong so she can fix it
She is concerned with other people's perception of her
They ARE the Joneses
She often projects her dreams on child/children
She is often boastful and arrogant

5. Codependent Mom

Her kids are her identity
She uses guilt to manipulate
She is afraid to be unloved or alone
She lives in a fear and scarcity mindset
She worries about what others think of her
She doesn't make decisions without input from others
She is hiding
She is afraid to be seen or let her light shine; fears failure
She doesn't want to outshine her kids/feels her time has
passed
She needs a lot of attention

She has big dreams but doesn't take action unless someone does it with or for her
She doesn't takes responsibility for her own actions
She compares herself to others
She puts herself in vulnerable positions
She often settles for less than she deserves/feels unworthy
She stays in her comfort zone
She embraces the role of martyr/plays the victim

6. Mindful Mom

She is a creative/out-of-the-box thinker
She knows who she is
She takes impeccable care of herself
She is fully self-expressed and integrated
She allows her child to be fully self-expressed
She nurtures the spirit of her children/praises their uniqueness
She sees each child as an individual
She upholds strong boundaries
She balances work and play
She is inclusive of all of her children
She has an open communication style
She shows emotion and models what vulnerability and connection look like
She admits when she's made mistakes
She is not attached to expectations or outcomes
She embraces every experience as a learning opportunity
She doesn't pretend to know it all
She listens to her child and honors their thoughts and experiences
She feels whole and complete within herself
She encourages fantasy, creativity, and experimentation
She openly expresses love and appreciation

Worksheets

Throughout this book I have provided contemplative questions and exercises that will assist you in your Awakening process.

Download your worksheets at ***www.MotherhoodsNotfor Punks.com/bonuses*** and revisit them as many times as you need to gain clarity.

Contemplative Questions:

1. Which of these archetypes do you feel most resembles your motherhood style?

_____

_____

_____

_____

_____

2. How do you think this motherhood style is affecting your child's confidence and self-image?

_____

_____

_____

_____

_____

_____

3. What inner conversations (stories) could be in the process
   of being created in them?

_____

_____

_____

_____

4. Is this style of parenting empowering or disempowering
   to your children?

_____

_____

_____

_____

_____

5. On a scale of 1–10 (1 = poor and 10 = fantastic), how
   would you rate your relationship with your children?

_____

_____

_____

_____

_____

Chapter 14

Mindful Mothering

-14-

Mindful Mothering

*"Motherhood provides the most joy and heartache
you'll ever experience in your life. It's the war
ground for learning what love, acceptance, trust,
forgiveness, and compassion really mean."*
- Patrina Wisdom

There is no perfect mother, so let it go and commit to being
the best mother you can be. Motherhood takes practice.
Unfortunately, our little loves don't come with instructions.
So, as with anything else, we need to learn how to be the
best parent to our children that we can be through trial and

error, reading books, and finding out what other parents are doing that seems to be working.

Release all guilt, shame, and regret in regard to motherhood. There's no room for it. Holding onto it weighs you down and drains your energy. The fact is that you're going to fuck up. It's what you learn from fucking up that matters.

Stop focusing so much time, energy, and attention on trying to be a perfect parent, and start focusing that same time, energy, and attention on being a present parent—present to your child's needs, their unique gifts, their communication style, their fears. The more present you are to your children's experience, the faster you will be able to notice, interrupt, and reprogram developing patterns and belief systems.

While it is our job to provide food, shelter, and clothing for our children, our innate desire as kids (and adults, for that matter) is to be seen, heard, acknowledged, and supported. So our greater responsibility as parents is to create for our children feelings of being safe and nurtured.

Honoring their thoughts, ideas, emotions, and needs models for them how to do it for others. Remember that we are not just raising little kids; we are raising future leaders. So it's important for them to be confident, develop communication skills, learn how to think for themselves, and make decisions. They will learn life skills and coping tools by watching you. So work on being the best you possible. This is what I like to call Mindful Parenting.

*"**Mindfulness** is a state of active, open attention on the present. When you're mindful, you observe your thoughts and feelings from a distance, without judging them good*

or bad. Instead of letting your life pass you by, mindfulness means living in the moment and awakening to experience."

– Psychology Today. https://www. psychologytoday.com/basics/mindfulness

So how can you bring more mindfulness into your parenting style?

Well, motherhood as a whole is a very broad topic. There are so many things that I could address, but I want to speak to the things that I feel often get overlooked. I will share as much as I can about mindful mothering in this chapter, but the conversation around each point is so vast that each topic could be a book in itself.

The Power of Presence

Something as simple as stopping what you are doing to look your child in the eye when he/she is talking creates the feeling of presence. If you want to take it a step further, kneel down to their level and look them in the eyes. Undivided attention and eye contact are by far the best ways to make anyone feel seen and acknowledged, which creates deep feelings of worthiness and gives children permission to take up space in their lives.

There are times when my children will come running into the room while I'm in the middle of a conversation, working on something important, or interacting on social media and I'm not able to fully listen to them. I simply tell them to pause and give Mommy a second to complete my thought so that I can give them my undivided attention. Something as simple as that little gesture will cultivate respect for your time and space. It will make them feel that what they have to say is important and that you want to hear them. And it gives them an opportunity to refine their approach in the future.

Speaking of undivided attention and social media, when you choose to be intentional about managing presence, you will want to have guidelines in place for technology and communications as a whole—for both your kids and yourself.

Some of the things I have in place include keeping my telephone ringers and notifications off or on vibrate at all times so that I'm not disrupted or distracted by every incoming call, notification, or message. This not only allows me to be more present with my children, it helps me to stay focused and get more work done throughout my day.

As an entrepreneur I set business hours, and I request that family and friends don't call me during these hours because I won't be available to talk. I also let my kids know when I'm working so that they can respect my time and space during those time blocks.

As far as the kiddos and technology are concerned, I put hours of operation on the phones and technology. In my home my kids can't use phones, play games, or watch videos on YouTube before 11:00 a.m. or after 7:00 p.m. Phones and/or games are not allowed at the table while eating. And I require my kids to look me in my eyes when they talk to me, as I do with them.

Kids are emotional creatures, and being present doesn't mean that you have to sit and be present with your child through every temper tantrum or emotional breakdown. What it does ask of you is that you acknowledge their emotions, give them permission to feel them, and then decide whether or not you want to participate.

There are times when my six-year-old comes downstairs with temper tantrums, tears, and hurt feelings because his big brother won't let him play Minecraft. In that moment my boy is distraught. He is in pain. The world feels like it is coming to an end because he can't play Minecraft!

I simply tell him, "I'm sorry that Ajani won't allow you to play right now, but it is his phone. You had a few tablets to play games on in the past and you broke all of them, so now you have to wait until Ajani is ready to share."

This is, of course, met with an intensified whine and the beginnings of a crying fit, so I just tell him to pause and I explain that he has every right to feel his feelings, but that he needs to do it upstairs in his room. So I look him in the eyes and I explain that he needs to take responsibility for breaking his tablet and to understand that Ajani is being nice by allowing him to play at all. Just like that his perspective shifts, the crying stops, and he runs up to wait his turn. You have to be present when your child speaks in order to listen, hear, and identify the real issue.

Active listening

Are you a good listener?

What is a good listener?

Are you hearing what you want to hear, or what your children are saying?

Does your relationship with your child/children reflect the answers you have given?

Your child's words may be saying one thing but their volume, tone, and body language could be saying another. Watch them when they speak so that you can pick up on the words or feelings that they are not expressing to you, often because they just don't know how. As mothers we have to learn how to read between the lines. It's easy to listen to what our children are saying, but are we really hearing them?

Be interested in what your kids are saying. Encourage them to expand on what they are trying to communicate to you. Ask questions like "Can you tell me more?" or "And then what happened?" Restating or repeating what your child says back to them will help you gain clarity as to what they want or need from you.

"So what you're saying is _____ and it made you feel _____, right?"

Next, you want to validate what they have shared (whether you agree or not) by saying something like "I can see how this is difficult for you" or "I can see that you are really angry about this." The practice of naming emotions will help teach your children how to identify and name their emotions as well.

Once you have a better idea of what your child is trying to communicate, you can shift a negative situation to a positive by reframing the situation. Reframing helps move them from blaming to owning their own feelings and taking responsibility for future outcomes.

I modeled this in the example about my son having a tantrum when he couldn't play Minecraft. Through reframing the situation, I was able to shift him from blaming his brother and calling him selfish and mean to him taking responsibility for breaking his own tablet, and respecting the fact that his brother was being nice by sharing his device. Before sending him back upstairs, I asked him a series of questions to ensure that he received the lesson.

Presence + Active Listening = Teachable Moments

In order to develop leaders we must teach our kids how to connect the dots.

When your children are asking you questions about something, don't be so quick to answer. It's great that you know the answer, but telling them the answers all the time is not serving them. Empower your children to use their own brains sometimes, and let them know that it's okay if they get the wrong answer as long as they try.

In situations where you've told your children twenty times not to do something and explained why, but they still do it, that's your cue to take a step back and let them learn the lesson the hard way. Just be there to lovingly help pick up the pieces if or when they crash and burn.

This will strengthen their deductive reasoning skills. It will build their confidence when they are successful at figuring out their own answers on their own, and when they get the wrong answer, it's a chance for you to step in and teach them a lesson. The paradox is true: success will never come without failure. Give your children space to fail forward and learn some lessons on their own.

Body Language

Body language is another aspect of communication to be aware of. Eye contact, smiling, open vs. folded arms, facing your children, kneeling down to talk to children at their level, and physically turning your body toward them when you speak are all positive and affirming ways to interact with your children.

I don't know about you, but I am very aware that many of my disempowering inner conversations came from my parents' interactions with me. Sometimes it was the words that they said, but more often than not it was less about what they were saying than it was how they said it.

When I was little, everything that came out of my mom's mouth sounded like she was fussing at me, so I walked on eggshells all the time and tried my best to be perfect so that I wouldn't have to hear her mouth (ha-ha, love you, Mommy). Her communication style made me feel like I was always being judged and that nothing I did was good enough. My hair, my weight, the way I made my bed and cleaned my room even, everything.

My dad, on the other hand, was a man of few words (at least to me), so I never felt comfortable talking to him about anything. I felt like he wasn't interested. Now of course, none of this was true, but that is how it felt. My mom and dad didn't set out to make me feel unworthy; they just weren't conscious of how their words and actions were affecting me.

After reading this book, you won't have that excuse. I am empowering you with the tools that you need to be a more conscious and mindful parent. And being conscious doesn't mean that you won't mess up or screw up your kids (ha-ha), but you'll have done your best under the circumstances.

Just put yourself in their shoes. Treat them as you want to be treated. Listen and acknowledge them in ways that you want to be listened to. But don't love them the way you want to be loved. Take time to find out what their love language is and love them in the ways that they receive love.

The 5 Love Languages

In the book *The 5 Love Languages* by Gary Chapman, he shares that there are five different ways that people feel and receive love:

1. Words of Affirmation
2. Quality Time

3. Receiving Gifts

4. Acts of Service

5. Physical Touch

He says that how you like to give love is usually how you like to receive it. So when it comes to your children, pay attention to how they show their love for you. Do they tell you how much they love you all the time? Are they the type of children that want to spend time talking and doing stuff with you, like playing games or watching movies? Do they make or buy you gifts all the time? Do you have kids that want to make you breakfast and serve it to you, or who offer to help with the dishes? Maybe you have one like my little guy who can lie on me and cuddle and kiss all day long?

I highly recommend reading Chapman's book so that you can take a deeper look at these love languages. I could never do it justice. (Keep in mind though that the book was written to address and strengthen relationships with our love partners and significant others.)

I have found that the information in his book has helped me in all areas of my life and in relationships: personal relationships, business relationships, and my relationship with my kids. Again, you have to think outside the box. Books about business can be translated to you as the CEO of your home. Books about relationships can help strengthen your bond with yourself and/or your kids. Information is information and everything affects everything. The common denominator in everything you do and experience is YOU. So work on YOU and everything else will fall into place.

Show up powerfully in your kids' lives

Remember that YOU set the tone of the household, so lead by example. Your kids will do what you do more often than not. So if you see something in your kids that you do not like, ask yourself the following questions before pointing the finger at them.

Where do I see this in me?

How can I love myself—and them—through this?

What can I do to shift this behavior?

I provided the tools needed to identify and manage your own stories, fears, and insecurities earlier in the book so that you don't project them onto your kids. Do whatever it takes to maintain your peace, no matter what's going on around you.

This is when your sacred self-care, morning rituals, and intention setting will serve you most. Having a regular practice will ground you energetically and arm you with the patience and energy that you need throughout the day.

Make decisions from an empowered space

Lean in and listen closely because I really want you to get this:

New Decisions Create New Realities!

No matter what you're faced with in life or business, always make your decisions from a place of clarity and abundance, and focus on the upgraded reality that you want to create.

Never make decisions when you are stressed, afraid, or in a scarcity mindset. It will always result in bad decisions, decisions that will create more of the same old reality that you are moving away from.

Play & Celebration

Give yourself permission to have fun! Far too many moms get so caught up in tending to the household and their kids and they forget and/or don't make time for play and celebration.

Life is not meant to be a series of tasks and to-do's. There is no reward for how many things you check off your list. Slow down! Take time to acknowledge each and every accomplishment.

You work so hard, so why aren't you taking time to celebrate your success? Learn to really be with it, feel it, and savor it, no matter how big or small the triumph is. This sets a great example for your kids to be on the journey of life rather than just pummeling through it.

Balancing masculine and feminine energy

I am probably writing this portion of the book more for my single mothers than anyone. Because we are playing the role of mother and father, nurturer and provider, and we have a tendency to blur the lines of our masculine and feminine energy. This isn't something we do consciously, and until we are made aware of it, we don't even know that we are doing it.

So let me explain what I mean when I reference your masculine and feminine energy.

Masculine energy is typically very singly focused on a specific mission or goal. It is a very assertive energy that is influenced by the primal instinct of survival.

Feminine energy is the life-force energy. It's the nurturing energy, typically influenced by emotions, connection, and flow. It's relaxed and flexible.

When you're a single mom, there are times when it serves you to be in your masculine energy—like when you're working to bring home the bacon, negotiating deals, disciplining your children, or dealing with auto mechanics and/or contractors. This all calls for unwavering conviction and strong boundaries.

Times when your feminine energy may be more of service include dealings with your kids' teachers, interacting with other parents, dating, and of course, nurturing your children. These are the times in our lives that call for more connection, compassion, and flexibility.

Balancing these two energies is a constant task for single mothers because we don't have anyone to step in and take a stand for us. We have to stand for ourselves. And if we aren't careful, this habit of taking a stand—and getting shit done on our own—can shoot us in the foot.

Many of us end up unconsciously creating an impenetrable fortress for ourselves because we have tilted too far into our masculine energy. We get so used to doing everything that there is no space for a man (or anyone else, for that matter) to step in and support us. It becomes an automatic response to just do it ourselves, and this does not serve us in our relationships or life because life is about collaboration and co-creation. It's an exchange of energy; therefore, we must always be giving and receiving.

Food for thought, my friend. I learned this one the hard way, so I invite you to start taking notice.

What areas of your life can use more of your feminine magic?

What areas of your life could use more of the masculine assertiveness?

Teamwork makes the dream work

One of the things I commonly notice in many families is a hierarchy of power inside the home, and to a point, I guess we need that. But what I've been playing with in my home since losing my husband is creating a team culture instead, one in which everyone has a voice, everyone is treated equally (with respect), and everyone has a hand in the running of the home.

I don't believe in paying kids to do chores. If we are a team, then everyone is expected to do their part to keep the home clean and functioning.

One of the most brilliant ideas that my husband contributed to our household when he was with us was the idea to create a family code of honor. A code of honor is a system, a set of rules, or ethical principles used to help govern a group of people or organization.

A code of honor is most commonly used as a system for governing businesses and organizations, but it makes sense to put one in place for your family too. After all, you are the CEO of your family.

Discipline

We had our older children memorize the code of honor, and when they did something that went against the code, we didn't make them wrong, or tell them that they were bad. We simply reminded them of our code of honor and pointed out to them why their actions were not serving them. Then I asked them what they thought their punishment should be for their crime. (You'd be surprised—they came up with some good stuff.)

Since becoming a single mother, I have found this way of disciplining my children far more effective and empowering for my children—not to mention that it is less energetically draining than yelling, spanking, punishing, and getting all worked up. I refuse to let these kids drive me crazy. I guard and stand strong in my personal power. When they do things that are out of line, I put the energy and responsibility on them. I hold them accountable for their actions. What a concept, huh? This is our job as parents: to teach our kids to use their brains, make decisions, solve problems, and be contributing adults and community members. The way to do that is to have and uphold personal and household boundaries and to function as a team.

All members of the team should know and be sold out to the dream.

When my husband was alive, the dream was to create a legacy of freedom for our family with our financial services business. Our dream now is to create a legacy for our family and help thousands of women around the world own their personal power and create their Badass Bodacious Life. It's a life of service and it's a total win-win!

You will always get more grace, mercy, compassion, and support when people know why you're doing what you're doing—the mission or motivation behind your actions. Involve your kids in your dreams. Find out what their dreams are. Let them play a part (or at least feel like they are) in the achievement of the goal or dream.

Share your pain and grief

If you hide your emotions and make things seem perfect all the time, your kids will feel pressured to be perfect and hide their emotions. It's important to model vulnerability and truth for our kids—not in the way of the martyr, but in the way of the Empress. The Empress owns all her light and all her dark, the beautiful and shiny parts, and the not-so-pretty shadow side of ourselves. Own it! Anything that is not truth is a lie.

I have found that my kids respect me more now that they know I am human. I allow them to see my struggle and my triumph because that's what life consists of. How better to teach them to overcome adversity than to allow them to witness it, and/or be a part of it?

Experiences vs. Stuff (values)

It is more important now than ever that we spend intentional time together as a family without distractions: television, social media, etc. Our society has become so consumed with everything that's going on outside ourselves that we have lost connection with ourselves, our kids, and others. It's taking the "human" out of "humanity."

So how can we combat this when it's so easy to just give your kid a game or put them in front of the TV? I say strengthening your relationship is the answer.

Below are some ideas on how to do that. Find what works for you.

1. Plan for weekly family dinners. Have them on the same day of the week and at the same time. During this time they will have your undivided attention and vice versa (no technology).

2. Family reading time. Take turns reading aloud from a book of choice and discuss what's happening in the story. During this time they will have your undivided attention and vice versa (no technology).

3. Date night with each kid. Schedule a day a month to spend time with each of your children individually so that they feel seen, heard, acknowledged, and loved. During this time they will have your undivided attention and vice versa (no technology).

4. Family meetings in which you pass a talking stick around the circle and whoever has the stick has the floor. The stick holder has the freedom to share anything that is up for them without judgment or repercussion. This creates a sense of safety and encourages your children to speak their truth (respectfully, of course). Any ground rules or guidelines would be discussed and agreed upon before entering into the sacred circle. During this time they will have your undivided attention and vice versa (no technology).

5. Family fitness—yoga, hiking, etc. A family that plays and stays fit together stays together. Not only will you be nurturing your relationship with your children, but you'll also be creating active, health-conscious children.

6. Family meditations, prayer, or spiritual study time. Don't just shove spirituality or religion down their throats; teach them how to use it. It could even be fun to help your kids create their own sacred space for meditation or an altar of their favorite things.

These are just a few ideas that have worked for me. I'm sure that you can come up with lots more. It's not about what you do; it's about how sacred your time is together.

"External circumstances will never create internal results. Internal results will always create external circumstance."
- Patrina Wisdom

In a world where everything moves so fast and where there are so many distractions, it's important to STOP and just breathe! Mindfulness is a practice of being present. Present to what's happening in your body. Present to your feelings and how you are affecting others. Mindfulness invites you to acknowledge the beauty that exists in your life now, rather than being stuck on the things that happened in your past or worrying about what will happen in your future.

Mindful Living is truly the Key to Awakening Health, Wealth, and Happiness. We create our realities with every thought, every word, and every feeling that we experience. Mindfulness brings you present to those experiences, and gives you the opportunity to redirect and recreate your life. Mindfulness opens you up to receive ALL of the love, joy, and wealth you desire.

Wisdom's Guide to Mindful Living From A to Z.
Download yours NOW! :
www.MotherhoodsNotforPunks.com/bonuses

Chapter 15

Raising Spiritually Gifted Children

-15-

Raising Spiritually Gifted Children

This chapter is a contribution from my magical unicorn friend Alison Elsberry.

Your child wasn't born to fit in. Your child was born to create a whole new world! They are extraordinary. You feel it. You know it in your heart. Maybe you already suspect your child is here for a big purpose, but perhaps you don't know what that is or how to help fulfill it.

Your child was born with distinct spiritual gifts we all need if we want to evolve into a more peaceful and loving planet. And when you recognize his or her behaviors as clues to their most meaningful talents, a whole new world of potential opens up for both of you. You start to decode the language of your child's soul, which is essential for empowering their lifelong potential.

And here's a little secret …

Your child sends you clues every day about who they are, but they can be easy to overlook and misunderstand. So how can you recognize those behaviors as spiritual gifts?

Here are a few hints. Your child may be …

- Highly intelligent yet struggling in school
- Extremely creative with passionate energy moving in every direction
- Strong-willed … maybe even rebelling against the rules
- Hypersensitive to other peoples' emotions, energy, and the environment
- Able to see and sense things beyond the physical plane
- Fascinated by concepts like faeries, magic, outer space, etc.
- Able to communicate with spirits, angels, and other nonphysical beings
- Drawn to world religions or spiritual masters
- Able to recall past lives
- Emotionally sensitive yet unable to express his or her feelings
- Intuitive and capable of knowing things out of the blue
- Exhibiting explosive reactions that seem to come

from out of nowhere
- Showing signs of natural healing abilities, like using his or her hands to comfort other people, animals, or dolls
- Playing with stones, crystals, and other spiritual healing tools
- Wanting to spend all their time playing in nature
- Highly inquisitive with insatiable curiosity
- Able to speak with a wisdom far beyond his or her years

Your child's latent potential is already activated and developed, and your awareness keeps their gifts open and alive. Their gifts need to be honored and acknowledged because that's what gives our spiritual leaders of the next generation the confidence to use them wisely.

So open your eyes, and be in awe. Acknowledge what you see and accept the gift that they are because to truly nurture their gifts and talents, you must be open to receiving the fullness of their spiritual expression—even when it feels scary, looks weird, and is frustrating. Or when you're at a complete loss for words, freaked out, and desperate for answers trying to understand their behaviors.

You raise your child into their fullness by validating their spirit through the Divine experiences and expressions they share with you. Saying "I see you" or "Tell me more ... I'm curious" and even "thank you" or "I love that about you" can be some of the most empowering energy your child *ever* receives. It's like a paintbrush to the canvas of their self-esteem, promoting a deep inward acceptance and encouraging them to reach their higher potential in life.

Feeling seen and heard is essential to the human spirit. And when your child learns to embrace their spiritual essence and feel good about who they are, the world instantly falls in love with them too. Your child is a blessing to the world, and they are here to share the magnificence of their being.

Now, keep in mind it may not look like you think it will … or should … or even the way you want it to. In fact, that's part of the mystery and magic left up to the Divine.

Maybe your child is destined to use their gifts standing on stage sharing an important message. Or perhaps they'll be a brilliant inventor, artist, musician, or visionary leader. Who knows, they may even be a master healer or a best-selling author.

What matters most is who they are right NOW. In this moment. And nurturing what shows up right in front of you. That's what helps shape their future and gives them the confidence to keep stepping toward the unseen and unknown.

Imagine what the world would look like if you, as a mother, stepped out of the way and let your child be who they came here to be and do what they came here to do. At some point, you must loosen your grip and let go. You can't force, push, or hold back God-given abilities and talents. The abundance of Spirit is meant to be shared with others. So resist the urge to control, fix, or make choices for your child.

Instead, trust.

Hold them lightly so that their soul's craving for freedom is satisfied, so that instead of fighting in power struggles, there's peace for both of you.

Your child's spirit needs breathing room with courage so that they can learn how to be in the world and not of it. So that they can learn how to be embodied with healthy energy boundaries and a clear connection to their heart's wisdom.

They are equal-level master souls and want to receive the fullness of who they are, instead of feeling obligated or like they owe anyone or are owed anything. Your child desires to show you how liberated they already are.

So leave the "planning" up to Spirit. Be willing to let them choose their own life—the one they're destined to have. And please remember, your presence matters. You have great influence with your child. In fact, you're the first impression of life that they receive, and the first relationship they ever experience begins with you.

You're that powerful!

Showing up and being present to whatever your child is expressing is *enough*. Listening is loving. Your presence has the ability to shift energy instantly ... just by being yourself. So when you find yourself worrying or being concerned about how their behaviors might be judged or criticized, why not say "thank you" and instead call attention to how brilliantly they experience the world through the eyes of their soul?

Your child IS different, and sometimes that will push you and others beyond what feels comfortable. So *expect* the BEST for you and your child. Ask for the miracles that have been set aside for both of you. And be open to learning, un-learning, and re-learning about who you are as a woman and mother. After all, you're raising a spiritually gifted child, and that requires changing how you see yourself and the world.

Enjoy the journey ... mess and all.

Give yourself a hug and embrace YOUR differences, and you'll find your child's extraordinary gifts will be easier to love too. I promise you'll find the sweet spot of your soul, and harmony will be all that exists for both of you.

Chapter 16

Relationships, Dating, Sex & Motherhood

-16-

Relationships, Dating, Sex & Motherhood

This particular topic is so vast that I could write a separate book about it (maybe I'll do that). But for now I'm just going to share some very important tips.

Tip #1 – You are the priority in your life. The hierarchy is God/Spirit, YOU, your partner, and then the children.

I know many of you are looking crazy right now, but this is the natural order. Anything else will throw you and your romantic relationship terribly out of balance.

Tip #2 – Schedule separate date nights with yourself, your partner, and each kid so that no one feels left out. (I told you this shit wasn't for punks.)

Tip #3 – If you are married or in a relationship, do not withhold or use sex as a bargaining chip or punishment. You will completely sabotage your relationship.

Tip #4 – Worship the one you love (or the one you're with, depending on your situation) and allow them to worship you. A great way to do this is to take turns. Alternate the planning of date nights and have the person making the plans be the worshiper on that night. The person whose night it is to be worshiped is also the person whose pleasure (orgasm) is the priority.

Tip #5 – Learn to speak your truth, ask for what you want, and come to agreements. The better you communicate with your partner, and the better boundaries or agreements you have in place, the better your relationship will feel.

Tip #6 – Single moms need to discover a fine balance (sometimes through trial and error) when it comes to exposing your children to partners. I've learned the hard way that it's not good to keep your partners away from your kids completely because when it gets serious, the transition is harder. Kids have a hard time accepting someone they haven't had a chance to bond with like you have. It can be very abrupt and may catch them off guard; therefore, they're more likely to reject the person. On the other hand, I would not advise you to introduce your partners too soon either.

What works for me is to ask myself the question, "Is this someone I want as a friend?" Believe it or not, this question will filter a lot of your partners out in a heartbeat. I don't know about you, but I have amazing, magical, supportive friends, and not all the men that I've dated in the past fit that description. They were hot as all get out, the sex was brilliant, and we had fun, but many of them are not people I'd bring around my amazing friends, so I definitely wouldn't bring them around my children. I know it sounds harsh, but I'm just being honest—honest with you, and honest with me.

As a single mom, there are times when we just want companionship, or an orgasm (that is not self-induced), or to have a beautiful dinner that we don't have to cook or buy for ourselves. So to this I will just say be mindful. Be safe. And don't ever neglect your responsibilities as a mother for a partner, especially if they are not one that you see bringing home to the kids.

Transition is a part of life. Not all relationships are going to be forever. It's okay to have fun. Just be clear about what the relationship is, and be honest with yourself (and them) about who is a playmate and who is a potential life partner.

Tip #7 – Make yourself easy to be found. Don't sit at home and wish for a partner and not follow it up with action. In order to be found, you have to be seen. Get out every so often for a meal or gathering with friends. Find ways to meet new people. Sign up on an online dating site. Release any attachment to specific outcomes and just be open to what shows up for you.

Tip #8 – Take ownership of your sexual power. Masturbate regularly (whether you're in a relationship or not). Learn to love yourself so that you can teach others how to love you. Learn to pleasure yourself so that you can teach others how to pleasure you. Don't make them guess and then blame them when they are not doing something right. Do what is needed to release all guilt, blame, shame, and regret related to sex, pleasure, and being completely liberated in the bedroom. Play games with yourself, and make it fun!

This is probably an overshare, but oh well, why stop now?

I like to set the scene for myself. I light candles, burn some incense, put on some sexy music, have a glass of wine. Then I gently caress my skin while sending love to each and every curvature on my body. When I'm primed and ready to go, feeling sensual and fully in my body, I begin my sacred practice of masturbation.

Using my fingers and/or toys, I make a game of it by seeing how many orgasms I can give myself; how deeply I can relax, release, surrender, and allow myself to experience pleasure. I also like to experiment with giving myself different kinds of orgasms.

Did you know that as women we have the capability of enjoying five different kinds of orgasms? Let me enlighten you.

1. Clitoral Orgasms
2. Vaginal or G-spot Orgasms
3. Cervical Orgasms
4. Anal Orgasms
5. Combination

The practice of masturbation can be transformational. It can help to build your confidence in and out of the bedroom, and it can free you of all your inhibitions around sex and sexuality.

Chapter 17

Creating & Cultivating Community

-17-

Creating & Cultivating Community

The days of women being catty and in competition with each other are gone. It's an old played-out paradigm that doesn't serve us as women. We live in an abundant Universe. There is plenty of money and men and beauty to go around. The only way to grow stronger as women and as a community, the only way to move humanity forward and raise incredible kids is to realize that we are all reflections of each other. It takes a village to raise a child. It takes a village of beautiful reflections of yourself to remind you of your strength and your beauty in the moments when you forget.

One of the most valuable lessons I've learned since packing up my kids and moving to San Diego where I had no family or friends is just how important it is to create and cultivate community. When you've lived someplace for a long period of time and you have family and friends there, it's easy to take it all for granted. But after floating in and out of Las Vegas for my entire life, it was time for me to go. I needed a fresh start, and I was willing to do whatever it took to get it—even though it meant leaving the village that had been so supportive to me.

You have to have that kind of conviction when you really want something. You have to be willing to take risks and make sacrifices. There is no playing it safe. There is no staying inside your comfort zone. In order to have Big Change, Big Transformation, and Big Reward, you have to make Big Sacrifices.

So how do you connect with like-minded women and create community?

Here are some tips:

Tip #1 – Know thyself. If you know who you are and what your needs are, you can seek out like-minded people to spend time with. Remember, your reality is shaped by the influence of the 5 percent of the people you spend the most time with, so choose wisely.

Tip #2 – Secure reliable child care. Use care.com or a babysitting/nanny service, or direct referral. When meeting other moms, you can offer to share your child-care provider and split costs or point her in the right direction. You can also take turns caring for each other's kids.

Tip #3 – Introduce yourself to your neighbors. Make the first move. Don't wait for them to talk to you. Find out who has kids. Invite them over for drinks or dinner. Be open to building relationships with the people who live closest to you.

Tip #4 – Get out and meet new people. Take advantage of the fact that you're the hot new face in town (or in the room). Choose one new place a week to check out, and go alone if you have to. A confident woman can go anywhere alone. I find that I usually meet the most interesting people when I do. Meetup.com is a great resource for meeting people because you can search activities according to interests.

Tip #5 – Be interested rather than interesting. Do your best to ask a lot of questions and learn as much as you can about the people you meet. Most people are so used to everyone talking about themselves and what they do that there is no time or space for the other person to share. Flip it. Be genuinely interested in learning about them, and then be open to share once they start asking you questions.

Tip #6 – Be of service. One of the best ways to meet great people is to align with a charity or outreach group that resonates with you. What better way to meet like-minded, service-oriented people?

Tip #7 – Find your peeps and cultivate a sisterhood. We all need connection. No one wants to feel alone. Long periods of disconnection can cause you to feel depressed, and it can diminish your self-esteem. Be proactive about aligning with other sisters to create circles of support, creation, and celebration.

Your community of support will not come to you. Someone has to initiate and create it. We all have obligations and demands on our time, so connection and sisterhood often get put on the back burner, but they're important and should be prioritized higher.

My sisters and I get together regularly to share our challenges and support each other, but we also spend a lot of time sharing our dreams and what we want to call in or create. Knowing and holding the intention for each other's dreams makes celebrating the accomplishment of the dreams that much more fun.

Acknowledgments

Wow! I can't believe the book is done! What a wild ride this has been.

I would not be the woman I am today, doing all the things I do, without the love and support of the following people.

To My Family:

First and foremost, I want to thank my incredible mother, Jerushia McDonald-Hylton, for her decision and commitment (at sixteen years of age) to be the best mother to me that she could possibly be. You have fulfilled your commitment and then some.

You have been my biggest supporter and have modeled for me what unconditional love, support, and Divine service look like. Things were not always perfect, but there was never a moment in my life where I questioned your love for me. Even when you don't agree with or understand the decisions I make, you still support me. You trust me as a Divine Spirit. You trust me as a woman and a mother. And you (should) have an unwavering inner knowing that you have equipped me with everything that I need to thrive in the world. There really are no words to describe my love for you.

To my dad, Bennie Washington, I love you so much, and I know that you love me to your core. We have spent this lifetime figuring out how to express our love to each other so that we can be blissfully bonded in the next. We have come a long way, Dad, and I look forward to deepening our connection and creating incredible memories together over the next twenty to thirty years of our lives. I see who you are to my kids, and I want you to know just how much I love and appreciate you.

Wow! Anthony Hylton, you have been such a light in my life. You have taken me into your heart as one of your own children and supported me throughout this journey. I am so grateful for and in awe of your love and generosity.

Ethney Green (my other mother), we have been on quite the journey together. From the time we met, you accepted me into your family as your daughter and the love of your son's life. Over the twenty-plus years that Alex and I were together, you and I became best friends. We enjoyed meals together, and we travelled together. We became so close that neither of us would consider making plans without consulting the other.

I'd like to thank you for your unconditional love and support while I was with Alex and for the love and support that you continue to provide in his absence. This transition has not been easy for any of us. I want to honor you for how graciously you have handled all the loss over the last six years, and to thank you for allowing me the space I needed to heal and to recreate. You will always have a special place in my heart and my life.

Suzi McDonald, how did I get so lucky? You have been my road dog my entire life. You have believed in me when I didn't believe in myself. You have loved me when I couldn't love myself. You hold me accountable to my greatness and call me on my shit when necessary. I don't always like it, but I appreciate the hell out of you and what you stand for in my life. Oh wow! Go figure ... as soon as I finished writing that sentence, my phone rang and it was Suzi, phoning to "call me out on my shit." Ha-ha! Don't you love the subtle synchronicities of life?

To my kids (Jorden Al'Hashim, Ramses Akbar, Ajani Akbar, and Taycuan Akbar), you are the reason I BE who I am and do what I do. My heart beats for you, and I want nothing more than to make you proud and to show you that you can do anything. Never place limits on yourself or try to fit into someone else's vision. You've seen me overcome every obstacle in my path over the years. You have the innate power within you to do the same. The publishing of this book is proof that you can create magic from chaos. I love you with every fiber of my being and am so honored that you each chose me as your mother.

To my two besties, Timeka Hall and Brian Pearson, you are the two people on Earth that know ALL my dirt (*shhh ...*), and you have been there to love me through all of it without judgment. With you I get to be Patrina rather than Patrina Wisdom, and that means so much to me. You are the sister and brother I never had, and I love you.

My Earth Angels:

Martha Demasco, you came into my life right after I lost Alex, and even though you barely spoke English, you saw my heart. You had a unique ability to reach into my soul and know exactly what I needed, even when I didn't know myself. Sometimes it was a look or a smile. Other times it was a hug, a shoulder to cry on, or a moment to myself. In the time that you worked in our home, you saved me. You healed me. You and your family were the glue that helped us put back together the pieces of our life. Your love and support helped heal my children. We are forever grateful to you and your family for your love and support.

Laila Ghattas of Aziza Healing Adventures and Laila Goddess Clothing, I am so grateful to you for our time together in Bali, which is where I learned the value of self-care and having compassion for myself. Thank you for your light and for always holding space for my kids and me. Our many retreats together and the retreat you facilitated for my family were pivotal to our collective healing. We have done some big work together, friend, and I am grateful to be on this journey with you. It feels good to know that no matter where I am in the world or what I'm doing, my Laila Goddess is tapped into my spirit and waiting in the wings to support me. I have eternal love for you.

Christine Essex of Luminosity Wellness Center of Las Vegas, NV, from the moment I met you, I knew you were an angel. Thank you for introducing me to the world of NLP (neurolinguistic programming) and helping me move through my disempowering beliefs and blocks. Thank you for helping me see that life doesn't have to be *either-or*; it can consist of *and*'s. You helped me lay the foundations for everything I've done and created in the years following our work. My mindset was forever shifted. My NLP training and certification changed my life, and our friendship has enhanced it in ways that I didn't know were possible. I love you.

Anne Cunnan Menik of Anne Holistic Health, I have you to thank for deepening my experience of spirituality that resonated with my soul and for the practice of yoga. You helped me move the feelings of grief through and eventually out of my mind, body, and spirit. You exposed me to spiritual practices, cards, and meditation. You acted as my healer in my time of transition and have become a treasured friend. I love you.

Ben and Tomoko Affleck, I have always been in awe of how you show up for people. You are angels to many, and I want you to know how much I appreciate the many ways that you have shown up for me, Alex (when he was alive), and for my family. You did everything from bringing over food, babysitting, taking my kids to activities, and more. Your value system, your integrity, your love, and your support made a huge difference in our lives.

Cynthia Andrews and Shakeitha Barlow, through our relationship with Ben and Tomoko, we were blessed with an extended family that really knew how to show up and support in times of tragedy. Your family's generosity will never be forgotten. There are always tons of people who show up to offer condolences when someone passes away, but you and your family continued to bring over full meals and called to check on us for months after the tragedy. You touched my soul.

To the *Motherhood's Not for Punks* Team:

Melissa V. Andrews, project manager, thank you for strapping on your seat belt and riding with me on my creative crazy train. You believe in me and my work and are so committed to helping me reach more women. I honor you, I thank you, I trust you, and I love you.

The 3 Amigas PR Team:

Jorden Al'Hashim (my daughter), no words, baby! I am so proud of the woman that you have become. You are such a powerful support to me in so many ways, and you inspire me daily with your grace, beauty, intelligence, and your pure heart. You love your mama, and Mama loves you! I feel super blessed to be able to create and serve together. Thank you for owning your Queenship!

Katy Fetko and Ali Lebo, I could not have attracted two better interns if I tried. I am so grateful for your level of commitment to me and the mission of my companies. It's been an honor to have you on the team. Your talents for media outreach and social media marketing are invaluable. I look forward to building even greater success together. You are both so talented and sweet. I'm excited to watch you grow and develop in your lives and careers.

Jolie Dawn of Jolie Dawn Consulting, you have been the creative inspiration behind this project. You saw in me an area of power and a potential for service in the world that I had taken for granted. Had you never sat me down and talked to me about how unique and powerful my motherhood style was, this book and the #Bams movement wouldn't exist. It just goes to show that our gifts are so often unrecognizable because they come so naturally to us. You are such a light, my friend, and I am honored to be a part of your empowered, sexy, and free life.

Andrew Reed of Andrew Reed Photography, thank you for being my go-to videographer and photographer on this journey. Working with you was a fun and **über** creative process, and we produced magic together. My Publishizer video and new marketing photos are DA BOMB!

Jerry Metellus for years of love, support, and friendship and for that incredibly powerful black & white image on the back cover of the book. I love you!

Robbin Simons and the team at Crescendo Publishing, thank you for providing all the support that I needed to push out the best book possible. Our work together flowed with ease, and I felt confident and supported along the way. We did it!

Tyler Benjamin Wagner of Authors Unite, you were my silent book publishing angel throughout this process. We have never met in person, but you watched me from the sidelines (Facebook) and offered the perfect words of support, inspiration, praise, and resources throughout the process of creating this book. I appreciate you and how you show up in the world. I can't wait to meet in person.

Flor Valdivia, my friend, nanny, and homeschool helper, I could not accomplish half the things that I do without you. You have become a part of the family, and we love and appreciate you very much.

Soul Sisters:

Diahnna Baxter, Kristina Italic, Christina Dunbar, Laketria Cornelious, Lisa Garcia-Ruiz, Andrea Currie, Patty Hayes, and Hayley Hunter Hines.

Thank you for holding me through the tears and growing pains of expansion and visibility. Thank you for believing in me and in my message. Thank you for preordering my book, sharing on social media, and checking on me throughout the process to see what was really going on behind the scenes. You kept me going and reminded me of why I had to finish this book and get it out to the world.

Diahnna Baxter and Christina Dunbar, thank you for inspiring me to do a crowdfunding campaign. You have both done them and know how tedious and beautiful they can be. You became my models for the campaign's success. I am so grateful to you for leading the way.

Diahnna Baxter, thank you for tapping into me and for following your guidance that day when Spirit told you to call me. You helped me see the beauty in the breakdown. I'm not sure that I would've had the strength to complete the campaign if it weren't for the perfect timing of your call. I love you, cousin.

How does it get better than this?
How did I get so lucky?
Namaste

Resources & Suggested Reading List

The Secret, Rhonda Byrne
The Ten Commandments of Self-Esteem, Catherine Cardinal, PhD
The 5 Love Languages, Gary Chapman
The 7 Habits of Highly Effective People, Stephen R. Covey
Intimate Communion, David Deida
You Can Heal Your Life, Louise Hay
Think and Grow Rich, Napoleon Hill
Rich Dad Poor Dad, Robert Kiyosaki
Change is Power, John Ross
The Four Agreements, Don Miguel Ruiz
The Power of Now, Eckhart Tolle
Until Today, Iyanla Vanzant

About the Author

Patrina Wisdom, Author | Speaker | Movement Leader
www.PatrinaWisdom.com

After losing her husband of twenty years to suicide and learning that she was pregnant with her fourth child on the same day, Patrina Wisdom took two decades of experience as an entrepreneur and business leader and began the process of Awakening Life.

She made the tough decision to awaken her life by walking away from the financial business that she and her late husband spent twelve years building to pursue a career that revolves around her passion for empowering and supporting women.

Fast-forward six short years: Patrina is a thriving mom-preneur, published author, and a dynamic speaker that has graced the stages of Lisa Nichols, eWomen Network, and TedX, just to name a few. She offers insight into transformational self-discovery that empowers women and mom-preneurs to move into purpose, create work-life balance, and let nothing stop them from creating their Badass Bodacious Life!

Her visionary work allows her to travel the world, inspiring others through her Wisdom Teachings, inspired parenting techniques (including homeschooling, mindfulness, and meditation), and her feminine model of entrepreneurship, and leaving CEOs and mom-preneurs feeling acknowledged, encouraged, and equipped. She wants to do the same for you.

Connect with Patrina

Book	https://www.facebook.com/Motherhoodsnotforpunks/
Facebook Profile	https://www.facebook.com/patrina.wisdom1
Facebook Page	https://www.facebook.com/PatrinaWisdom/
Instagram	https://www.instagram.com/patrinawisdom/
Twitter	https://twitter.com/PatrinaWisdom
Youtube	https://www.youtube.com/channel/X0x9ZmAEPU1uEAiwZ6xfnA?view_as=public
Pinterest	https://www.pinterest.com/patrinawisdom/
LinkedIn	https://www.linkedin.com/in/patrina-wisdom-author-speaker-movement-leader-8b978829

Something a little silly for you...

https://youtu.be/UKYy-SfQQWI

Special Thanks to Contributing Author
Alison Elsberry

Alison Elsberry, Empowering moms to raise spiritually
gifted children
www.AlisonElsberry.com

A very special thank you to my magical unicorn friend
and contributing author Alison Elsberry for her incredible
contribution of Chapter 15, "Raising Spiritually Gifted
Children."

Alison has sixteen years of experience as a pediatric
occupational therapist and holistic health specialist working

with moms and children, and she's a clear channel for sharing the wisdom and teachings of Mother Mary. She has made it her mission to empower moms to nurture their children's spiritual gifts and soul talents, and it was such an honor and blessing to have her contribute her magic and expertise to this book.

The Journey to Publishing

Exactly four months ago I scheduled a personal writing retreat at the Danyasa Eco Retreat Center in Costa Rica to start writing this book. I chose Costa Rica because I wanted to be someplace quiet, simple, and tropical: all the things that I knew would be nourishing to my soul as I dove into my writing.

In the first seven days of the trip, I completed eleven chapters (rough drafts, of course), and then my girlfriend Kristina Italic surprised me by coming out to join me on the trip. We spent the last seven days of the trip playing, setting intentions, doing good witch magic, and calling in all the things that we wanted to create for ourselves upon our return home.

While in Costa Rica, everyone I met and spoke to had a word or a message for me that confirmed that I was on the right path, and I gained access to many resources I needed to make the book successful, including a chance meeting and connection with one of the sexiest, sincerest, most open-hearted and vibrant men I've ever met, Guy Vincent.

After hours of conversation at Mongo Congo Café in Costa Rica with Guy sharing invaluable tips and information on how to write and publish a successful book, I found out Guy is the creator of a crowd-publishing platform called Publishizer.com. Funny enough, I had already been considering running a crowdfunding campaign on another site, but after meeting Guy, there was no doubt in my mind that it was Divinely aligned for us to work together. It was actually in that conversation that the title of my book, *Motherhood's not for Punks*, came through.

Upon my return home, I began preparing the proposal for my crowd-publishing campaign. Within two weeks it was approved, and the campaign for the book was launched.

The crowdfunding campaign was one of the most exciting, expansive, and uncomfortable experiences ever. It provided me with an opportunity to move through an edge that I had around ASKING for and RECEIVING help. It tested my faith and trust in the power of the Universe, the power of community, and the power of my message.

The campaign launched me into a whole new level of visibility, allowing me to reach more people and touch more lives before the book was even released. In the end, our campaign resulted in 155 books pre-sold, and we raised $4,440 to use toward the publishing and marketing of this book. I am so proud of what we accomplished together.

Thank you, Guy Vincent, for coming into my life and offering the support, information, and platform to get my book out. I feel lucky to be able to call you my friend, and I am forever grateful for what your Publishizer platform has done for me. So much love to you!

Publishizer Crowd-Publishing
Patron Supporters

A very special thank you to all the following people who supported our
Publishizer Crowd-Publishing Campaign.

Big thanks to each and every team member on the following list for their financial contributions, social media shares, energetic support, prayers, love, and support. This book would not be possible without your help. I have never felt so held.

BOOK CAMPAIGN SUPPORTERS

Jerushia & Anthony -Hylton	Kathryn Goetzke	Lesley Wirth	Rae Majors-Wildman
Akili Hight	Katherine Zagone	Lynnean Chisom	Robin Windsor
Alison Elsberry	Hayley Hines	Ali Shanti	Helene Henager
Augusta Massey, Esq.	Ladonna Jackson	April Stickelman	Ron Williams
Andrea Shackelford	KeeKee Cornelious	Laura Swan	Sharon Franklin
Andrea Currie	LaTonya Washington	Janelle Bledsoe	Rose Mueller
Andrea Medina	Denita Grewer	Samantha Madhosingh	Ruthie Grunwald Edelson
Drew Reed	Diahnna Baxter	Adena Sampson	Rebecca Hegemier
Ashley Haggerty	Regina Bailey	Varant Majarian	Samara Holliday
Beth Walls	Dana Marshall	Makena Sage	Sandra Bland
Christine Essex	Flossie Park	Marsh Engle	Sheila Collins
Brian Pearson	Brenda Gallow	Denise Michaels	Kay Wilburn
Nancy Parker	Myra Surratt-Walters	Micole Noble	Sekou Andrews
Camille Macres	Ethney Green	Mitzi Reed	Leslie North
Carole Hurd	Greg Clowminzer	China Hudson	Michele Grier
Carrie Saba	Gay ThomasWilson	Anne Cunanan Menik	Shawn L. Duffy
Chandra McAtee	Guy Vincent	Nariha Serano	Shereen Thor
Christina & Chaim Dunbar	Hoda Ait Rahou	Natalie Vartanian	Stacey Ellen
Claytee White	Petra Fuerst	Patty Hayes	Stone Love
Catharine Chope	Jacki Beem	Patty Contenta	Susette Horne
Tiffany Goyer	Jackie Cobbs	Psalm Pollock	Sydni Sayles
Paulette Moreau	Jay Kamara Frederick	Priscilla Stephan	Tanya Paluso
Cory Michelle Johnson	Jazmine Henderson	Anthony Raboteau	Conni Pontuto
Dallas Cyr	Juliet Brown	Dharma Rose	Suzanne Highgate
Danielle Fields	Jessica Winer	Raquel Romero	Steve Erickson
Dean & Lisa Grafos	Jolie Dawn	Reba Labat	Robyn Tingley
Desiree Meza	Kathy Everett	Barborara Charles	Terri Bothwick

Alex Torres
Tyler Wagner
Renee Airya
Akira Chan

Diamond Patron Supporter – Shawn L. Duffy

A very special thank you to Shawn L. Duffy for her incredible show of support during the final hours of our Publishizer Crowd-Publishing Campaign.

In the last two days of my thirty-day crowd-publishing campaign, I was led by Spirit to surrender. I had been working around the clock for twenty-eight days in an effort to raise the money we needed to make the publishing of this book possible, but my spirit was guiding me to let go and allow myself to be supported by my angels and my community rather than pushing and forcing.

On the last night of the campaign, I booked myself into the La Costa Resort & Spa in San Diego for a day of relaxation and reflection. I knew that I had already done all that I could do to create momentum and awareness for the campaign, so I chose to trust that however things turned out in the end, it would be perfect.

While relaxing at the spa, I met two beautiful women in the hot tub. As we were laughing and talking, they began sharing their motherhood stories and challenges with me. I listened intently and shared a bit of my motherhood Wisdom, but I was reluctant to share more about my story or my book because I was supposed to be relaxing, and I didn't want to come off like a shameless marketer or saleswoman. Then Spirit reminded me that it would be a disservice not to share my story and my book with them. Turns out, I was the exact person that they needed to meet, and I had the exact words that they needed to hear.

It was such a blessed interaction that left one woman, Ginger Guarnieri, in tears of gratitude and prompted the other woman, Shawn L. Duffy, to jump out of the hot tub and run for her phone and credit card while yelling, "We're doing this! I want to buy 100 copies right now." I was in complete shock. By simply being willing to put my own inner conversation on mute and choosing to openly share what I was doing, we created a total win-win.

Shawn ended up supporting at the $850 Empower Level that night, which boosted our campaign funds tremendously, and she gave the Bonuses, which included a Complimentary Breakthrough Coaching Session and Complimentary admission to my Sacred Selfcare Retreat, to her friend Ginger Guarnieri.

We ended the evening by celebrating our new friendship with dinner and drinks. How does it get better than that?

Thank you so much for your support in getting this book in the hands of the women around the world that needed it. I am forever grateful for your fast action and generosity.

Made in the USA
San Bernardino, CA
30 April 2016